Rails Around Walsall

Yesterday and Today

One of the last Webb tank engines, 2-4-2 No.46701, takes water at Walsall on 7th May 1952, having propelled its train from Wolverhampton. The loco was on loan to Bushbury shed from Warrington (8B), whilst this train's usual motive power, 41225, was in works.

(F.W.Shuttleworth)

written and compiled by
JOHN BOYNTON

best wishes,
John Boynton

Rails Around Walsall

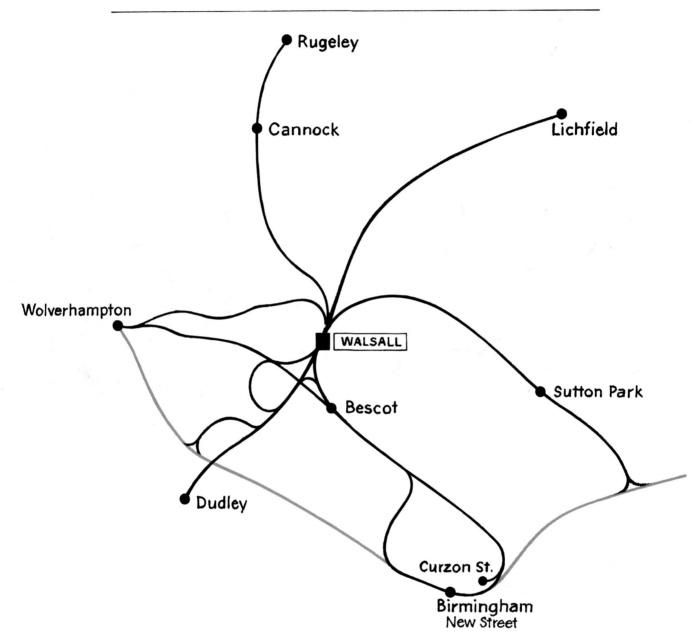

Rugeley

Cannock

Lichfield

Wolverhampton

WALSALL

Sutton Park

Bescot

Dudley

Curzon St.

Birmingham
New Street

Gresley A4 Pacific 60009 "Union of South Africa" takes the Walsall line at Bescot with a charter train from Worcester to Crewe via Nottingham, 3rd February 1996, Ray Churchill at the controls.

(John Whitehouse)

CONTENTS

INTRODUCTION

Although never mentioned in the same breath as Crewe or Swindon, Walsall is a significant rail centre. Its station is small and, despite recent improvements, the passenger service is still inadequate for a town of almost two hundred thousand people. No locomotives were ever built here; no great railway engineer was born here. Yet, when the London & North Western Railway opened a new engine shed and marshalling yard at Bescot in 1892, Walsall entered the railway age. The yard remains an important part of the modern railfreight network.

Little has been written recently about Walsall's railways and no book has been devoted to the lines radiating from the town. Having spent my early childhood within earshot of Bescot yard, "Rails Around Walsall" is an attempt to throw more light on a neglected story.

The Grand Junction Railway of 1837, with its Walsall station at Bescot, was one of the first main lines in the world. The South Staffordshire brought the added benefit of clean water to disease-ridden Walsall, piped alongside the tracks from Lichfield. The Cannock line spawned a spider's web of mineral railways across the coalfield, while the line through Sutton Park - briefly frantic with activity in the summer of 1957 - is still a busy freight route. The present day service to Birmingham, with four trains every hour, is more frequent than ever before.

My initial appeal for material produced a quantity of previously unpublished photographs and some useful written information. Many railwaymen were also keen to share their memories of Walsall's two rail centres, Bescot and Ryecroft.

This book does not claim to tell the whole story. The present situation is not all satisfactory and the future is uncertain. The long struggle to reopen the Cannock line to passengers was the first of many such battles. If other campaigns are also successful, the Walsall area can look forward to a much improved train service - eventually.

John Boynton
1996

A Class 86 Bo-Bo electric, 86008, hauls an eastbound mixed freight along the Grand Junction line on the approach to Bescot, alongside the M6, 18th July 1973.
(Michael Mensing)

CHAPTER ONE : THE GRAND JUNCTION

(A Pioneering Line : Problems and Innovations : Opening and Success : Amalgamation and Diversion)

A Pioneering Line

Most people, even if they have no interest in railways, will be able to remember something about their history as a result of lessons learnt at school. Many will recall the names of George Stephenson, the "Rocket" and the Liverpool & Manchester Railway. That line, the first to link two places of importance, opened in 1830. Although planned as a freight railway, it was an overnight success as a carrier of passengers - it had to be, as freight facilities were not ready for the first few months - and this stimulated the construction of other key lines, a few of which had been proposed for a number of years. Those that were serious enterprises had always fallen at the final hurdle when they failed to secure an Act of Parliament, without which no railway could be built. One such was a proposed line between Birmingham and Birkenhead (for Merseyside), Bills for which were rejected by the House of Commons in 1824 and 1826. However, the success of the Liverpool & Manchester Railway, and the reform of Parliament in 1832, began a change in attitude by the Establishment to the new form of transport. Important new lines now stood a more realistic chance of being built.

On 6th May 1833 the Bill for the London & Birmingham Railway received the royal assent and so became an Act. On the same day the Bill for the Grand Junction Railway also became law. The Grand Junction was a much modified version of the Birmingham & Birkenhead. The Birmingham terminus was to be at Curzon Street, alongside the London & Birmingham station, and the line would run north via Stafford, joining the Liverpool & Manchester near its mid point at Newton. The junction for lines to Chester and Manchester would be on a green field site, near the home of Lord Crewe.

It was fitting that this was the only British railway ever to have the word 'Grand' in its title. Providing a link between the London & Birmingham and the Liverpool & Manchester, it was to be the world's first trunk line. With a length of 77 miles, and an opening date targeted for the summer of 1837, it was to be the key piece in the jig-saw from which the national railway network would grow. George Stephenson was appointed Engineer by the Directors (none of whom came from Birmingham, as there was at first little interest in the town) in September 1833 at a salary of £2,000 per year. A month later Joseph Locke was appointed *"Engineer under Mr.Stephenson with the special care of the Liverpool end of the line but with the superintendence of the whole in the absence of, or when required by the principal Engineer, and that he be allowed a salary of £800 per year".* Locke had been George Stephenson's apprentice when only 18 years old. Prior to this new appointment he had been resident acting engineer for the whole line, with a salary of just £100 per year. Now aged 28, he possessed energy and enthusiasm in abundance. He recognised that this promotion could provide him with an international reputation as an engineer - and so it proved - so he quickly concluded all other commitments *"in order that my mind may be disengaged for the great work I am about to undertake",* rejoiced at the spectacular increase in his salary, *"this is beyond my expectations in every way",* and married his young fiancée, Phoebe McCreery.

Problems and Innovations

However, all was not idyllic. A rift between Locke and Stephenson, which had begun before Locke's appointment, developed as the line was built. At first the two men worked together in a spirit of co-operation but matters deteriorated within a year. Stephenson left no record of his version of events, Locke's unfinished autobiography was lost after his death. It appears, from the Directors' minutes, that Stephenson was less and less interested in the line, leaving Locke with virtually all the responsibilities of both men. Stephenson failed to make reports, he never attended meetings and letters from the Directors went unanswered. Despite his reputation, this could not be tolerated, yet the Directors - many of whom had been on the Board of the Liverpool & Manchester, which Stephenson had engineered so brilliantly - were reluctant to dismiss him. At the same time they recognised that Joseph Locke was more than fulfilling his own duties. They therefore appointed both men as joint engineers in November 1834. Only when Stephenson had continued to draw a salary for virtually no work for a further nine months did the Board's patience finally end, downgrading Stephenson to a consultant, with a retaining fee of £300 per year and promoting Locke to Engineer-in-Chief at a salary of £1,200. Stephenson resigned a week later.

It says much for Joseph Locke that this turbulence did not affect his lifelong friendship with Stephenson's son, Robert. The ending of his difficult relationship with George caused him to collapse with what appears to have been severe nervous exhaustion, unable to do anything for several weeks. Although determined to adhere to the opening date of summer 1837, the Board was as tolerant of Locke's illness as it had been of Stephenson's inaction. One of Locke's deputies, William Allcard, with his assistant John Errington, was left largely in charge of the works while Phoebe Locke coaxed and cajoled her husband back to health.

Whilst his relationship with George Stephenson had been deteriorating, during the summer of 1834, Joseph Locke had had to contend with a problem at the Birmingham end of the line. The original route would have involved a tunnel under rising ground in Aston Park, the land belonging to Aston Hall. James Watt, who lived at the hall and was the son of the famous engineer, strongly objected to a railway over or under his land. Locke went to investigate and was able to report that a route to the east would add only a mile to the line, the gradients would be trifling, the tunnel was no longer needed and the troublesome Mr.Watt, who had spent about £2,000 on his personal anti-rail crusade, could be ignored.

The Aston diversion, plus unbuilt branches to Walsall and Wednesbury, was sanctioned by an Act of June 1835. The new alignment required an embankment, and a viaduct spanning the Lichfield Road and Fazeley Canal. Aston Embankment was accompanied by a diversion of the Tame. A loop in the river was eliminated, confining its course to the north of the embankment and avoiding the need for the line to bridge it twice. At first the embankment was unstable, especially where it crossed the old riverbed and on one occasion the contractors had the misfortune

The Grand Junction
and associated lines

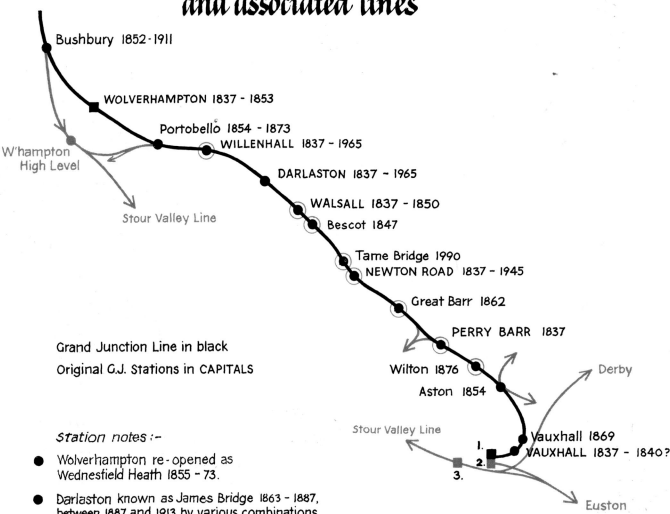

Bushbury 1852-1911

WOLVERHAMPTON 1837 - 1853

Portobello 1854 - 1873
WILLENHALL 1837 - 1965

DARLASTON 1837 - 1965

WALSALL 1837 - 1850
Bescot 1847

Tame Bridge 1990
NEWTON ROAD 1837 - 1945

Great Barr 1862

PERRY BARR 1837

Wilton 1876
Aston 1854

W'hampton High Level

Stour Valley Line

Derby

Stour Valley Line

Vauxhall 1869
VAUXHALL 1837 - 1840?

Euston

Grand Junction Line in black
Original G.J. Stations in CAPITALS

1. BIRMINGHAM (G.J.) 1837 - 54
2. Birmingham (L + B) 1837 - 54
3. Birmingham New Street

Station notes :-

● Wolverhampton re-opened as Wednesfield Heath 1855 - 73.

● Darlaston known as James Bridge 1863 - 1887, between 1887 and 1913 by various combinations of both names.

● Walsall re-opened as Wood Green (Old Bescot) 1881 - 1941. This was a new station on the original site.

● There were three stations on different sites at Newton Road — 1837-63 ; 1863 - 1902 ; 1902 - 45

● Great Barr is now known as Hamstead.

● Vauxhall is now known as Duddeston.

to see one section subside eight feet (2.5m) in an hour. Trouble with the embankment threatened to delay opening of the line, but Locke excavated an artificial pool nearby and the 20,000 cubic yards of clay and gravel extracted from that proved sufficient to stabilise it. Aston Viaduct, although mutilated, carries today's electrified railway over the same road, next to Aston station. Two arches were replaced by the girder bridge when the Lichfield Road was widened and Aston station is built on part of the viaduct. The bricked-up arches on the other side of the road are original. When the line opened the area was rural, so rural that it was not even provided with a station at first. Aston opened in 1854 and, as the urban area expanded northwards, Witton opened

to passengers in May 1876 and to goods in 1887. Aston Villa Football Club was founded in 1874 and Witton would have been the most convenient station for the ground, were it not for the fact that the club moved from a pitch in Aston Park to Perry Barr in the autumn of the same year. A new stadium in Aston, on the present site at Villa Park, did not open until 1897. An early guide to the Grand Junction, published in 1838, said that a little to the east of Aston Hall *are the quiet and retired village and church of Aston.*

The Grand Junction was successful, efficient and ready to adopt new technology, thanks largely to Joseph Locke. With an eye to economy and efficiency he experimented with a new type

Trains pass on Aston Viaduct, the parish church and Aston Hall visible on the left.

of rail, weighing 64lb/yard. Seen in cross-section it resembled an exercise dumbbell stood on end. It was his intention, once the running surface had become worn, simply to turn it upside down. In this way it would have double the life of a conventional rail. In practice the lower surface became dented and worn by the chairs on which it sat, making it unfit for use. Despite this failure, Locke was ahead of every other engineer of the time when he recognised that the most satisfactory way to lay a track was on sleepers. George Stephenson's track was laid on stone setts, like some ancient quarry tramroad; Brunel's broad gauge was laid on longitudinal timbers, with metal tie bars at intervals. Both types were difficult to lay, maintain and keep accurately in gauge, but both were still regarded as the only true 'permanent way' - sleepers were scorned, only suitable for temporary contractors' lines. However, the Grand Junction was the first line to be laid throughout with sleepers. Having abandoned the use of reversible rails, Locke's conventional rail weighed a hefty 84lb per yard and rested on chairs secured with wooden 'keys', the forerunner of bullhead track, whose use spread throughout the world. The weight and design gave a smoother, less rigid, less hard ride than on any other line. Only Locke was confident that this was good enough to be permanent way - the Directors were unconvinced. By 1845 just 20 miles of sleepered track remained, the rest had reverted to blocks. However, when he engineered the London & Southampton Railway in 1837, Locke again used sleepered track. This time it was permanent, ultimately sounding the death knell for stone blocks and Brunel's baulk road.

Unlike some early railways the Grand Junction was safe, carrying almost a quarter of a million passengers (232,202) in its first six months, without accident or injury. This was double the number travelling by road coach over the same route in the six months before the line opened. One area where the Grand

Junction was perhaps less successful - at least to modern eyes - was the way in which it failed to serve the towns along its route. The only place of any importance which had a station anywhere near the town centre was Stafford. The fourteen miles at the southern end of the Grand Junction linked Birmingham with Wolverhampton, the first of four routes between the two. It also served Walsall, after a fashion. The Birmingham station, a temporary structure at Vauxhall, was over a mile and a half from the Bull Ring, almost two from the new Town Hall. The permanent station at Curzon Street, opened in January 1839, was only marginally more convenient. The Wolverhampton station was at Heath Town, a mile and a half distant from St.Peter's and the central market area. This generated an advertisement from an enterprising inhabitant in the "Wolverhampton Chronicle" on 19th July 1837, six weeks after the line opened:-

"T.Smith begs respectfully to inform his friends & the public that he has commenced running an OMNIBUS to the RAILWAY STATION in time to meet the different trains. Swan Hotel, Wolverhampton."

The two stations were known simply as 'Birmingham' and 'Wolverhampton', accurate but suitably vague. The station described in the early time-tables as 'Walsall' would today fall victim to the Trades Descriptions Act. It was at Bescot, north of the present station, where the line crossed the Walsall - Wednesbury Road at Wood Green. The site is now almost underneath Junction 9 of the M6. A horse bus, timed to connect with the trains, ran between the station and the town some two miles away. Willenhall and Darlaston had more convenient stations, but Newton Road had an omnibus link with West Bromwich, almost three miles to the south-west.

It may seem surprising, in a local context, that Walsall was all but ignored by the planners of the Grand Junction. The railway by-passed Walsall for the same reason that it ignored West Bromwich and skirted round Wolverhampton. It was conceived as a direct freight link between the Midlands and the North-West. As locomotive technology was in its infancy, the route chosen went through the easiest country, keeping to river valleys wherever possible. As a result the line was cheap to construct, costing just under £1.5 million pounds for 78 miles, or about £18,840 per mile. This compared with over £35,000 per mile for the Liverpool & Manchester and £53,000 per mile for the London & Birmingham. These figures vary slightly according to the source consulted but, even without the need for a terminal station at the northern end, or engineering works such as Chat Moss or Kilsby Tunnel, the Grand Junction was inexpensive, although it did require some significant works.

The most substantial structure is Dutton Viaduct over the River Weaver in Cheshire, 1,400 feet long and completed in 1836 without the loss of a single life. Further south are two lesser viaducts at Aston and Lawley Street, on the approach to Curzon Street. There are only two brief tunnels on the whole line; that at Wednesfield Heath just south of the Wolverhampton station is 186 yards long. At 422 feet above sea level (described in an early guide as "422' above the level of low water at Liverpool") it is also at the summit of the line. To avoid substantial earthworks wherever possible, some gradients are steeper than any on the Liverpool & Manchester or London & Birmingham, except for the ascent out of Euston, which was cable worked at first. Evenso, there is nothing exceptional. The greatest challenge is for southbound trains tackling the six mile ascent of Madeley Bank in Staffordshire, never steeper than 1:177. The gentle rise northwards from the second class station at Perry Barr, at 1:502, is typical. As locomotive technology developed many subsequent lines with much steeper grades were laid with confidence. (The 1:37 Lickey Incline on the Birmingham & Gloucester Railway, opened in 1840, cannot be seen as part of this gradual progress, but as an act of reckless bravado in the quest for cheap construction.)

To propose a route through a town centre - any town centre - would delay construction and add considerably to the expense of the line, even without opposition from people who did not want any disruption from the new steam monster which they did not understand. The line's promoters reasoned that goods could easily be brought some small distance to the station yard by road. People who wished to travel by train would not be deterred by a road journey of one, two or even three miles to reach the nearest station. Both these points were at first perceived as fact. Ideas soon changed, and the convenience of rail travel generated demands for greater convenience. The station at Wolverhampton, although more convenient than any pre-rail facility, soon became inadequate for freight, leading to demands for a goods station nearer the town and its industries. The stations at Walsall (also known as Bescott Bridge) and Newton Road were quickly criticised by some who used them because of their distance from the towns they were supposed to serve. With no previous experience of long distance railway building to guide them, the planners of the Grand Junction had foreseen none of these disadvantages. They chose the best end-to-end line in every sense, but it soon became less than satisfactory for most places en route, particularly south of Wolverhampton. Proposals to build a branch line to Walsall as early as 1839 came to nothing, thanks to opposition from Edward Elwell senior, who owned Wednesbury Forge at Wood Green, and T.F.Wood, a Walsall magistrate. The branch had two influential supporters, Lord Bradford and Peter Potter Esq., but Potter changed sides suddenly. Did any of this

have anything to do with the fact that Potter and Elwell's sons were about to be appointed as county magistrates, the site for the town station would take some Elwell land, or that the existing station was inconvenient for almost everybody - except Wednesbury Forge?

In the early 1850s a second line between Birmingham and Wolverhampton was constructed by the London & North Western Railway. It opened fully in July 1854, with new town centre stations at Birmingham (New Street) and Wolverhampton (High Level). This line is still mistakenly called the Stour Valley, after a projected branch leading from it, which was never built. It is the route taken by today's InterCity trains between Birmingham, Manchester and the North West, joining the old Grand Junction just south of Stafford. It makes no pretence of serving Walsall.

Opening and Success

Prior to these developments the Grand Junction, in the nine brief years of its independent existence, provided a benchmark for measuring the progress of railways in general. It opened for passenger traffic on 4th July 1837, which was the exact intended date when construction had begun almost four years earlier. It was also fourteen months before the London & Birmingham line was completed. The Grand Junction opened without ceremony at the request of the Directors. The country was still supposedly in mourning for William IV, 'Silly Billy', who had died on June 20th and whose funeral did not take place until July 8th. More importantly, some Directors had been at the opening of the Liverpool & Manchester when the "Rocket", driven by Joseph Locke, had accidentally run over and fatally wounded the Liverpool MP, William Huskisson. He, along with many others, had been moving freely on the line partly because of poor crowd management, and Locke in particular wanted no further accidents in similar circumstances. This did not stop large crowds gathering to witness the first train, particularly at Birmingham and Wolverhampton. It left the temporary Birmingham station at Vauxhall at 7am, eight named first class carriages hauled by a Robert Stephenson built 2-2-2 loco, No.8 "Wildfire", which weighed under 10 tons. Thousands lined the route as the train - which would seem puny indeed to modern eyes - accelerated to 30 mph over Aston Viaduct and 40 mph through Newton Road. The number of spectators grew during the day, so much so that one train from the north, due to arrive at Vauxhall at 2pm was delayed by the number of excited people near the track between Wolverhampton and Darlaston, noted in company records as *the obsterperous intrusion of the workers from the iron and coal districts*. All subsequent trains were also heavily delayed, the last two arriving at Vauxhall in tandem at 3am the following morning. This, and the fact that the second northbound train failed to stop at Wolverhampton *owing to a misunderstanding on the part of the engineer* (driver) were only minor irritants; the world's first long distance railway was open for business. The following day's "Wolverhampton Chronicle" expressed great satisfaction *at the successful completion of an undertaking of such vast interest to this trading and manufacturing district*. Like the Liverpool & Manchester before it, the Grand Junction was not ready to receive goods traffic when the line opened, so all revenue had to be earned from passengers. There were about 65 first and second class carriages, plus fifteen third class open trucks. The estimated 200 goods vehicles would not be needed until February 1838. The carriages were too small for passengers to stand upright inside so the luggage on the roof - plus the occasional passenger - remained well within what was then a generous loading gauge.

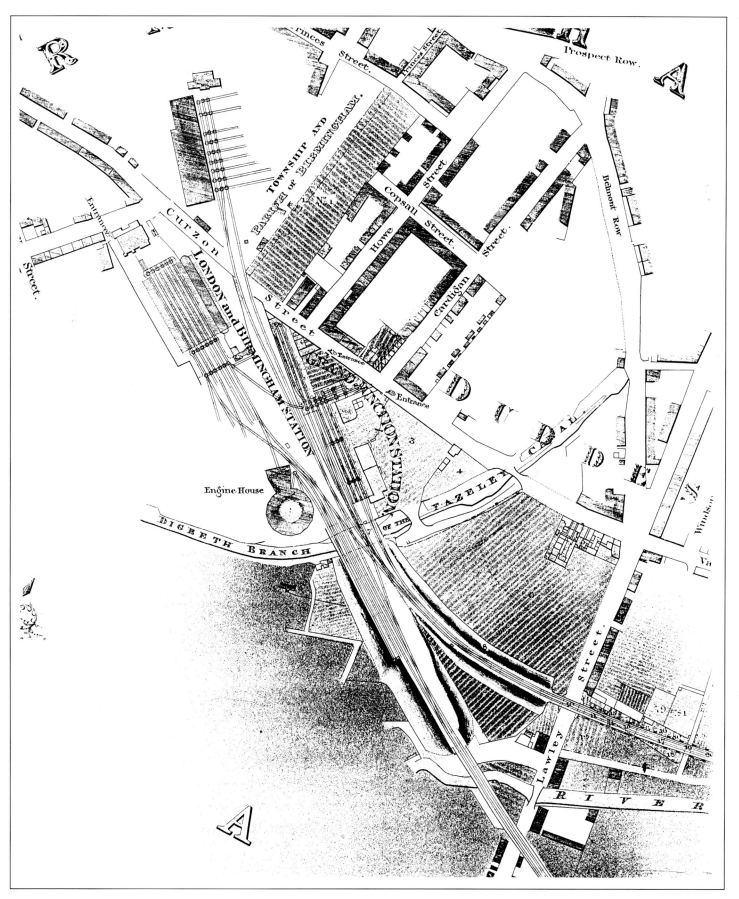

Map showing the two stations at Curzon Street, Birmingham, 1839. It is full of interesting features, including the Lawley Street viaduct, the rail link between the two stations, the goods station, the L&B roundhouse and carriage and wagon turntables, useful for quickly disposing of what were then very short wheelbase vehicles. The fields show that this is still the edge of the country. Taken from an 1839 'elephant' folio (23"x28") mapping the entire route in colour. *(Public Record Office, Kew, ref: Rail 220/33)*

The initial train service was such that the stud of small but reliable locomotives was called upon to work intense schedules and high mileages. It is recorded that in the twelve weeks following the opening, July 8th - September 30th 1837, "Wildfire", which had hauled the first train out of Birmingham, ran 11,865 miles. "Scorpion" at 11,137 miles and "Shark" at 10,018, were not far behind.

The temporary terminus at Vauxhall had pillars to support the roof but no side walls for protection against the weather. It served as the Grand Junction's most important station before the Lawley Street Viaduct was completed. As well as cheaper and quicker travel, the railway brought other advantages. All but the poorest inhabitants of Birmingham, Wolverhampton and Walsall could benefit from an improved and more varied diet. The speed and capacity of the railway made it possible, for the first time, for large quantities of fish from Liverpool docks to reach the Midlands still in a fit condition to eat. The Grand Junction was the first railway to sign a contract with the Post Office, setting a precedent that others soon followed. It carried mail from the opening day. Not content with merely providing mail vans, a railway horsebox was soon converted into a Royal Mail sorting carriage, the first in the world. It was first used on the 7.15pm mail from Vauxhall to Liverpool on 6th January 1838, the same month that the line opened for general goods. Mail bags were also taken on board at Walsall and Wolverhampton. Sorting mail on the move helped speed up the process of collection and distribution, the experiment was successful and in September of the same year purpose-built mail vans entered service. They were fitted with mailbag exchange apparatus, which could discharge and collect bags at speed.

The Grand Junction was complete with the opening of the 28-arch Lawley Street Viaduct in January 1839. This gave access to the Curzon Street terminus, alongside the London & Birmingham station. Trains were timed to connect with each other and through tickets were issued. Even before the line was complete the GJ train service was completely recast, in October 1838, to connect with that of the L&B via a special omnibus link between Vauxhall and Curzon Street. (Vauxhall closed on an unknown date, probably before the end of 1840 - company records offer no clue. A station on the present site at Vauxhall did not open until 1869.) Both Curzon Street stations had even been built by the same contractors, Grissell & Peto.

The Grand Junction terminus buildings, in use only for goods after 1854, were demolished in June 1971. They died as a result of indifference. The "Birmingham Post" (23rd June 1971) quoted Councillor Harold Edwards, Chairman of Birmingham Public Works Committee, as saying that the city had not realised their importance until it was too late. A British Rail spokesman added "the preservation order applies only to the part of Curzon Street with the Ionic arch" (the London & Birmingham station) "we were therefore able to go ahead and demolish the hall".

An early time-table, reproduced from "Bradshaw's Railway Guide" for January 1843, makes interesting reading. Places in capitals are first class stations, at which all trains normally stopped, and from which there were road coach connections. Trains at Wolverhampton, for example, were met by coaches for Kidderminster, Worcester, Dudley, Stourbridge, Shrewsbury and Ironbridge, already making the small station a busy transport interchange. Walsall was not quite as first class as the others, as both daytime mail trains did not stop, neither did some Sunday

GRAND JUNCTION.

Distances.	Up Trains. STATIONS.	3¼ a.m. London Mail *	6 a.m. Mixed Class	8¼ a.m. Mail	10½ a.m. Mail	4 p.m. 2nd Class	7 p.m. London Mail *	
Mls.	Trains Leave LIVERPOOL	3 30	6 0	8 15	10 30	4 0	7 0	..
19¼	WARRINGTON	4 17	6 55	9 2	11 20	4 55	7 47	..
22½	Moore	..	7 3	..	..	5 8	..	..
25	Preston Brook	..	7 16	..	..	5 16	..	..
29¼	Acton	..	7 30	..	..	5 30	..	..
31¾	HARTFORD	4 53	7 40	9 38	11 58	5 40	8 23	..
36¼	Winsford	..	7 56	..	..	5 56	..	..
38¾	Minshull Vernon	..	8 2	..	..	6 2	..	..
43½	CREWE	5 24	8 23	10 9	12 32	6 23	8 54	..
46	Basford	..	8 32	..	..	6 32	..	..
51½	Madeley	..	8 52	..	..	6 52	..	..
54¼	WHITMORE	6 5	9 5	10 50	1 15	7 5	9 35	..
62½	Norton Bridge	..	9 25	..	..	7 25	..	..
68¼	STAFFORD	6 37	9 45	11 22	1 47	7 45	10 7	..
72½	Penkridge	..	10 6	..	..	8 6	..	..
76	Spread Eagle	..	10 15	..	..	8 15	..	..
77½	Four Ashes	..	10 19	..	..	8 19	..	..
83	WOLVERHAMPTON	7 18	10 36	12 3	2 32	8 36	10 48	..
85½	Willenhall	..	10 50	..	..	8 50	..	..
88	WALSALL	7 25	10 59	..	2 40	8 59	10 55	..
90¾	Newton Road	..	11 9	..	..	9 9	..	..
94¼	Perry Bar	..	11 19	..	..	9 19	..	..
97½	BIRMINGHAM	8 0	11 30	12 45	3 15	9 30	11 30	..

FARES

Between Liverpool and Birmingham.

	£	s.	d.
Four Inside Coach	£1	7	6
Six Inside Coach by Mail Trains	1	6	0
Six Inside Coach by other Trains	1	4	6
Second Class Closed Carriages	0	18	0
*Third Class Open Carriages by 6 a.m. train from Liverpool, and by 6 a.m. train from Birmingham	0	13	0

*Passengers will be booked by this conveyance from Liverpool and Birmingham to First Class stations only, and from First Class stations to either of the Termini, but not to intermediate stations, at lower rates in proportion.

Children under Ten years of age half-price.
Ditto in the arms, free.

	£	s.	d.
One Horse	£2	0	0
Two Horses, if one property & in 1 box	3	0	0
Three ditto	4	0	0
Dogs, each	0	3	0
Gentlemen's Carriages, Four Wheels	3	0	0
" " Two "	2	0	0
Passengers in Private Carriages at 2nd Class Fares	0	18	0
Grooms in charge of Horses, if riding with them in the box	0	14	0

Sunday Trains.—1st class leave Liverpool for London, at 3 30*, Mixed 8 15 a.m. and 7* p.m. (10½* a.m. to Birmingham only), stopping at first class stations only.

To London by the following trains:—On week-days, at 8¼ and 10½ a.m. taking first class passengers, and horses and carriages. 7 p.m taking first class passengers only.—On Sundays the 8¼ a.m takes first class passengers, and carriages and horses; and the 7 p.m first class passengers only.

NOTICE.—Passengers should be at the first class stations 5 minutes and at the second class stations 10 minutes, before the time specified.

A supply of Trucks and Horse-Boxes will be kept at all the principal stations on the line; but to prevent disappointment, it is requisite that notice should be given at the station where they may be required, the day previous. No charge for landing or embarking Carriages or Horses on any part of the line.

Trains marked thus * stop at Walsall station for passengers proceeding to Birmingham or Stafford, or other first class stations north of Stafford.

(Courtesy of Central Trains)

trains. Lesser stations were served only by slower trains and there was just one train each way which carried third class passengers, the 6.00am from Liverpool and the 6.00am from Birmingham. The latter started as it meant to go on, taking 15 minutes to cover the 3 miles to Perry Barr. It was possible for the wealthy to take their horse(s) and carriage with them, the animals travelling in a horse box with the groom, the carriage secured to a flat truck.

A certain C.S.Greaves travelled from Worcester to Stafford three days after the line opened, "bringing the carriage I have hired with me on the Railway". He wrote to his sister in glowing terms about the experience -

"The pace is very steady and regular and never apparently too fast ..... We came from Birmingham here, 30 miles, in an hour and five minutes, excluding 7 minutes lost at Wolverhampton, and from that place 16 miles in 28 minutes. At present I am clear the rails are not properly settled, as in some places you clearly perceive a jar at each junction and in others a lateral motion. It certainly is a delightful method of getting over the ground and no-one, I should think, having once travelled by it would trouble horses again if he could avoid it. You see but little of the country, partly by reason of the rapidity, but chiefly owing to the low level of the rails, which in many places almost touch the brooks they pass. The seats and tickets all being numbered there is little confusion about places and the luggage is piled on the top of the vehicles. I have no doubt many improvements may still be made, but I think it is good enough as it is."

Thomas Moore, travelling from Vauxhall in 1838 wrote-

"(I) was quite enchanted with the swiftness and ease of the course. There I sat, all the way, lolling in a most comfortable arm-chair and writing memorandums in my pocket-book as easily and legibly as I should at my own study-table, while flying through the air at the rate of thirty miles an hour."

If these accounts seem a little too good to be true, perhaps they are. Most third class passengers were illiterate. Not one of them has left any known record of the delights of travel by open truck, which was the norm for this and most other railways before Gladstone's Railway Act of 1844 compelled them to be conveyed in covered vehicles at a minimum average speed of 12mph.

The Grand Junction was, without question, a successful main line. In purely financial terms it normally paid 10% dividend per annum to its shareholders, peaking at 15.5% for the first half of 1840. This was better than any other line at the time. For the first six months of 1845 the Chairman, John Moss, was able to announce that receipts for passengers and mails were £150,000, an increase of 50% above the same period in 1838. The increase in income occurred in spite - or because of - two fare reductions. Modern rail operators please copy! Freight traffic was more slow to establish itself, although the 1845 half-yearly income of £73,000 was much higher than for any previous period.

A southbound express from the Grand Junction line slows for the stop at Bescot, about 1903. The locomotive is Renewed Precedent 2-4-0 No.2178 "Pluck", withdrawn in September 1922. This photograph shows more clearly than most the relatively small size of these front rank express locomotives. They were highly successful, the 24inch cylinders, 6'6" driving wheels and high (for the time) working boiler pressure of 150lb/sq.in., ensured that a huge amount of energy was packed into a small frame. Had such a phrase existed in Edwardian days, they would have been described as 'turbo-charged'.

(Thomas Hinckley; Roger Carpenter collection)

Amalgamation and Diversion

On New Year's Day 1846 the Grand Junction, London & Birmingham and Manchester & Birmingham railways amalgamated to form the London & North Western Railway, an arrangement endorsed by Act of Parliament the following July. The LNWR built on these earlier foundations, expanded and prospered, styling itself the 'Premier Line'. The Grand Junction was a vital part of the enlarged system.

The Stour Valley line, with the advantage over the Grand Junction route of town centre stations in Birmingham (New Street) and Wolverhampton, opened fully on 1st June 1854. A local passenger service had begun two years earlier to the day, but full opening was delayed while New Street station was completed and a complex quarrel between the LNWR and the Shrewsbury & Birmingham Railway was resolved. This centered on the S&B claiming its running rights over the Stour Valley and the LNWR's determination to deny them. It descended into farce during the summer of 1853 when the LNWR began a lavish half-hourly local service so that it could claim that there were now no paths for S&B trains. The LNWR feared that the S&B was really an agent of its bitter rival, the Great Western, whose own route between Birmingham (Snow Hill) and Wolverhampton was also nearing completion. The S&B was indeed absorbed by the Great Western in September 1854, after which it ceased to have running rights over the Stour Valley line.

None of these antics affected the Grand Junction line directly, but between Birmingham and Wolverhampton it became less important as an express passenger route as soon as the Stour Valley opened. The GJ's Curzon Street station lost its passenger service completely and for ever. The new station at Wolverhampton had opened when the local service along the Stour Valley began in June 1852. It was at first known as Queen Street, re-named High Level in 1885 and reverted simply to 'Wolverhampton' when it became the only remaining station in the town centre in 1972.

Wolverhampton's small Grand Junction station was renamed Wednesfield Heath in 1852. A few expresses continued to use the original line after Queen Street was opened. They served Bescot and connected with Walsall trains. They ceased to call at Wednesfield Heath in May 1853 and the station closed in November of that year. Wolverhampton passengers on such trains were required to change at Bushbury, where the old and new lines met north of the town. (Bushbury closed in 1912, tramway competition having reduced income for the whole of 1911 to just £42!) A new station was opened at Portobello in 1854. Wednesfield Heath re-opened in 1855, but both these stations, together with the GJ line between Portobello and Bushbury junctions, were closed to passengers in 1873. The stations remained closed when the line itself re-opened to passenger traffic on 1st March 1881, although Wednesfield Heath remained open for goods and parcels until October 1965. Re-opening of this stretch was part of a package of improvements to LNWR lines in the area which brought some express passenger trains back onto this part of the Grand Junction and also improved the service at Walsall. 1st March also saw the opening of two spur lines, between Portobello and Heath Town junctions at Wolverhampton, and between Pleck and James' Bridge (later Darlaston) junctions at Walsall. A glance at the map will confirm that Walsall - Wolverhampton trains could use both these new sections for a straightforward journey, instead of the roundabout route via the Midland line through Short Heath. The Portobello - Heath Town link became more than locally important when the new line between Stechford and Aston was opened to passenger traffic exactly a year later, on 1st March 1882. It had opened to goods in the autumn of 1880, but the embankments were allowed to settle and a new station at Stechford, west of the original, was built at the junction. It then became the practice for Euston - Wolverhampton trains to divide at Stechford. The front portion went via Aston and over the Grand Junction, calling only at Bescot, before entering Wolverhampton via the Portobello - Heath Town link. The rear portion called at New Street and was then downgraded to a local service to Wolverhampton. This pattern worked in reverse for up trains. However, the revival was not permanent and the balance of long distance trains was to become heavily biased in favour of the Stour Valley route. Nevertheless the Grand Junction saw some regular express workings until the early 1960s, especially on summer Saturdays. A few of these trains served Bescot, including the named "Midlander", hoping to attract Walsall passengers, as when the Grand Junction first opened.

The local passenger service between Walsall and Wolverhampton was withdrawn in 1965 but the local service from Birmingham to Bescot and Walsall is busier than ever, with an off-peak frequency of four trains per hour since October 1995. However, apart from diversions, the Birmingham - Wolverhampton section of the Grand Junction now sees no long distance passenger trains. Nevertheless, because of its continuing importance as a freight artery, it remains an integral part of the West Coast Main Line and was electrified, along with the rest of the Euston - Birmingham - Liverpool/Manchester section, in the 1960s.

Most buildings dating from the days of the Grand Junction have now disappeared. Some survived until the 1960s and 70s, only to be swept away without much thought for their historical importance. The Wolverhampton station at Heath Town (named Wednesfield Heath) had buildings no larger than a cottage. It continued in use for goods traffic for many years after the passenger service was withdrawn in 1873. The LNWR built a substantial goods shed approached, from the south, via Railway Street. The cattle pens were near the 'to Birmingham' platform, reached via the original approach, Station Road. Other stations have come and gone within Wolverhampton since 1837, but this remains the only Station Road in the town.

The Birmingham terminus at Curzon Street was not in the style of its London & Birmingham neighbour, a scaled down variation of Euston's Doric arch which is now a listed building.

Advertisement from the pages of a guide to the Grand Junction Railway, 1839. *(courtesy of Central Trains)*

An un-named member of the "Jubilee" Class, No.45528, at Wolverhampton (High Level), having brought its Birmingham-Glasgow train over the Grand Junction through Bescot and Willenhall, a regular route for certain expresses until the end of steam. Photographed about 1961.

(Bob Lane)

Instead, the GJ station had a long and impressive stone frontage with four huge doors giving access to the platforms. Level with the door tops a frieze of nine large niches extended from end to end. Perhaps it was intended that they should be occupied by statues of famous engineers, in the manner of saints on a cathedral wall, but they remained empty. During the early 1840s, before it became apparent that the Curzon Street stations would not be able to cope with the rising volume of traffic, there were plans to extend New Street (the road, not the station) out from the town centre to the stations. This was never done, although some maps of the period show the line it would have taken. Nothing remains of the temporary station at Vauxhall, but next to the present day Duddeston station is an old brick building where engineers' rolling stock was repaired and maintained until 1994. This is the Grand Junction engine shed of 1840, a most important survival, still in railway ownership, although sadly no longer in use.

The track between Vauxhall and the New Street approach at Proof House Junction was raised in 1893, using a new viaduct over the busy throat of the Curzon Street goods stations. This was approached from the north via a new 'second storey' added to the Grand Junction's Lawley Street viaduct. Near the site of Newton Road station a bridge is still recognisable as one which

appeared in an 1837 engraving. The central arch was raised when the line was electrified and the parapet has been altered, but the stone abutments and two side arches are still in original condition. The stonework is in the same style as the portals of Wednesfield Heath Tunnel, now used only by freight trains.

The Stour Valley line was sanctioned by an Act of August 7th 1846, the same year in which the GJ became part of the LNWR. This Act authorised the diversion of the lines using the Curzon Street termini to a new through station at Birmingham New Street. On completion it was covered by what was then the largest roof in the world, constructed of glass and iron and weighing over 1,100 tons. It was 840 feet long, 75 feet above rail level at the apex and with a single shallow span of 212 feet. Twenty years later William Barlow's beautiful train shed at St.Pancras - still one of the sights of London - was 150 feet shorter and only 30 feet wider. E.W.Cowper, the architect of New Street's roof, had worked on the Crystal Palace for the Great Exhibition of 1851 as Joseph Paxton's junior partner.

In the same year as the LNWR was formed and the Stour Valley authorised - 1846 - steps were being taken to give Walsall a better place on the railway map......

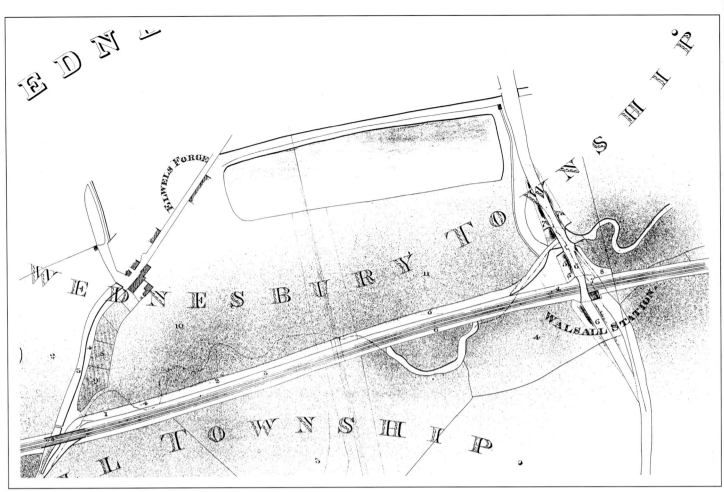

The Grand Junction's Walsall station at Bescot, 1839. The Wednesbury Road was diverted over a new bridge, which gave the station its alternative name of Bescot(t) Bridge. An unknown hand has defaced the original by pencilling in the route later taken by the South Staffordshire Railway.

(Public Record Office, Kew, ref: Rail 220/33)

A Webb 2-4-2 tank, bearing the LMS number 6704, pauses at Darlaston on the Grand Junction line with a push-pull train from Wolverhampton (High Level) to Walsall, 13th August 1947. The billboard nearest the loco is for use by the GWR.

(W.A.Camwell; Don Powell collection)

A picture of the working railway - grubby, outdated, inefficient, full of memories and nostalgia. An ex-LMS Stanier 8F 2-8-0 freight locomotive, No.48175, slows for a signal check with a northbound train at Perry Barr, 26th June 1957. Within ten years the station had been modernised, the road was widened and the houses were swept away. *(Michael Mensing)*

A Fowler 'Crab', No.42936, eases along the Grand Junction line through a murky Willenhall station with an eastbound steel train, c.1961. When Willenhall had two stations the London North Western one, seen here, was known as Bilston Street. *(Bob Lane)*

The South Staffordshire Railway

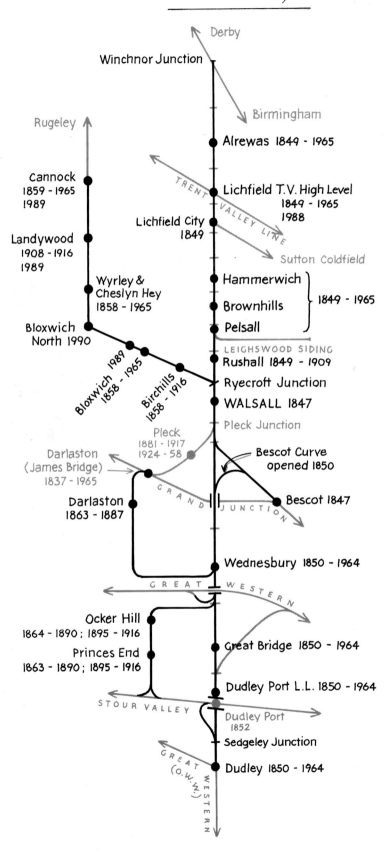

Derby

Winchnor Junction

Birmingham

Alrewas 1849 - 1965

Rugeley

Cannock
1859 - 1965
1989

TRENT VALLEY LINE

Lichfield T.V. High Level
1849 - 1965
1988

Lichfield City
1849

Landywood
1908 - 1916
1989

Sutton Coldfield

Hammerwich

Wyrley &
Cheslyn Hey
1858 - 1965

Brownhills   1849 - 1965

Pelsall

Bloxwich
North 1990

LEIGHSWOOD SIDING

Rushall 1849 - 1909

Bloxwich 1989
1858 - 1965

Birchills
1858 - 1916

Ryecroft Junction

WALSALL 1847

Pleck Junction

Pleck
1881 - 1917
1924 - 58

Darlaston
(James Bridge)
1837 - 1965

GRAND JUNCTION

Bescot Curve
opened 1850

Darlaston
1863 - 1887

Bescot 1847

Wednesbury 1850 - 1964

GREAT   WESTERN

Ocker Hill
1864 - 1890 ; 1895 - 1916

Princes End
1863 - 1890 ; 1895 - 1916

Great Bridge 1850 - 1964

Dudley Port L.L. 1850 - 1964

STOUR VALLEY

Dudley Port
1852

Sedgeley Junction

GREAT WESTERN (O.W.W.)

Dudley 1850 - 1964

(Walsall's Own Railway : John Robinson McClean, Engineer : Out On The Line : Expansion & Absorption : Everything In Duplicate : Fuel For Thought)

A Super D, LMS No.9861, with a long mixed freight train - consisting mainly of wooden-sided, private owner coal wagons, passes over Cartbridge Crossing on the South Staffordshire line as it heads towards Ryecroft Junction. The LNWR signal post shows the Ryecroft distant arm at caution. The upper arm was worked by the crossing keeper, under the direction of Rushall box. The crossing cottage is almost hidden by the engine. Living accommodation for the crossing keeper, her platelayer husband and their children, was one large room. They kept about three dozen fowl and, in best railway tradition, never needed to buy fuel as lumps of coal 'fell' from passing trains manned by their friends. Photographed from the Sixty Steps Footbridge during the summer of 1934. *(Frank Ash)*

Walsall's Own Railway

The South Staffordshire Railway, with its headquarters at Walsall, was an important line serving the heart of the industrial Black Country and the South Staffordshire coalfield. Its main line, 23 miles long, ran from Wichnor Junction in the north, through Lichfield and Walsall, to reach Dudley via Great Bridge and Wednesbury. It connected with the Great Western at Dudley and Great Bridge; with the LNWR Stour Valley line at Dudley Port; with the Grand Junction line at Bescot and with the Birmingham - Derby main line of the Midland Railway at Wichnor. This connection with the Midland meant that the South Staffs provided the most direct link between the industrial areas of the West and East Midlands. The line was of more than passing interest to the London North Western and Midland railways, both of whom saw it as a means of extending their influence into each other's territory.

The South Staffordshire was first promoted as two separate concerns, the South Staffordshire Junction Railway (Dudley to Walsall) and the Trent Valley, Midlands & Grand Junction Railway (Walsall to Wichnor). The latter company's inflated title was more than mere pomposity; the potential importance and strategic nature of the route was recognised by the fact that it had a provisional committee of no fewer than 42 Directors, four of whom were MPs, including George Hudson, York's 'Railway King'. The Act authorising these lines, passed on 3rd August

1846, gave them powers to amalgamate. This they did the following year, mercifully reducing their combined name to 'South Staffordshire Railway' and culling the Directors to a more workable maximum of 18, all of whom had to hold a minimum £50 worth of shares. The Earl of Bradford was given £100 in shares as an inducement to sell some land needed for Walsall station. Among those who had supported the idea of the line from the beginning were Charles Smith Forster, Walsall's first MP following the 1832 Reform Act, and both the Edward Elwells, father and son, of Wednesbury Forge.

The first section of the South Staffs to be opened linked Bescot with a temporary station at Bridgeman Place, Walsall, a distance of a mile and a half. John Bagnall of West Bromwich had successfully tendered to supply the rails (1,000tons @ £9.92/ton) and their chairs (250tons @ £6.92/ton). The train service began on 1st November 1847. There were four trains per day in each direction, two in the morning, one late afternoon and one mid-evening. All ran between Curzon Street and Walsall, calling at Perry Barr, Newton Road and a new station at Bescot Junction. The single fare was 1/6d (7.5p) first class, 1/- (5p) second, with no apparent provision for third class passengers. The Curzon Street - Walsall third class fare, at a legal maximum of one penny (1d) per mile, would have been 11d (4.75p) so the second class fare was hardly excessive. Return tickets were 2/6d (12.5p) first class and 1/6d (7.5p) second. Parcels weighing less than 15lbs were carried by passenger train for just 4d (2p), including delivery! The first and last weekday trains also ran on Sundays in connection with trains to and from London. As the company had no rolling stock of its own at first, these trains were operated by the LNWR.

The junction at Bescot was about half a mile nearer Birmingham than the Grand Junction's 'Walsall' station, which reverted to the name of Bescot Bridge. Passengers between Walsall and the Wolverhampton direction were conveyed between Walsall and Bescot Bridge by horse bus until the latter station closed in 1850. This would suggest that the new Bescot station was not able to serve both lines at first.

The South Staffs was seen by the Midland as a way of extending its influence into the Walsall and Dudley area; it was seen by the LNWR as a way of reaching Dudley, the Midland line to Derby and, of course, the centre of Walsall. In addition, Dudley was perceived as a frontier town in the battle between the standard gauge and Brunel's broad gauge, as used on the Great Western. The Birmingham Wolverhampton & Dudley Railway (BW&D) - only nominally independent of the Great Western - received sanction from Parliament to build a line between Birmingham and Wolverhampton. With the Grand Junction and Stour Valley, this would be the third line linking those towns and at first it was broad gauge. (Formerly part of the Great Western main line linking the West Midlands with Paddington, most of the route is now occupied by Line 1 of the Midland Metro, which it shares with the Jewellery Line at the Birmingham end.) The Act for the BW&D was passed on the same day as that for the South Staffs. It authorised construction of a broad gauge branch from Swan Village to Dudley if the South Staffs had not built and opened their line to Dudley by 1st November 1849.

This threat to the integrity of the South Staffs meant that the three groups on its board worked together while it lasted. Roughly one third of board members represented LNWR interests, one third the Midland, and one third were independent shareholders. Building the line continued apace and the 17 miles between Walsall and Wichnor opened in 1849. The date is often given as 9th April, but all that happened then was the running of a special for Directors, followed by a celebratory lunch at the George Hotel, Lichfield, attended by the mayor of the city and the High Sheriff of Staffordshire. Passenger services for ordinary mortals had to wait until 1st June. That day saw the opening of a permanent station at Walsall, on the present site. Other stations were at Rushall, Pelsall, Brownhills, Hammerwich and Lichfield (just north of the present City station). A South Staffs station at Lichfield Trent Valley opened in August, eleven months after that on the main Trent Valley line below. The Midland had running rights to Walsall and the LNWR had running rights through Wichnor Junction to Burton and Derby, capital of the Midland system.

At first there were four trains daily between Walsall and Burton, operated by the Midland, the LNWR providing the Walsall - Bescot shuttle, with connections to/from Curzon Street. This was all well and good, but the failure of the South Staffs to devise its own operating regulations from the beginning caused problems which could have been avoided. Before 1859, for example, there was no rule book, as the South Staffs borrowed from its neighbours. Most company servants used the Midland book, except for drivers, who used the LNWR book! When the South Staffs rule book did appear, it advised that guards were *"forbidden to pass over the tops of the carriages when in motion and anybody doing this without urgent necessity will be fined"* and that, *"goods trains must not run over the line .... at furious speeds"*.

South of Walsall, the track to Dudley was almost complete by 1st November 1849 but several months' work remained on the stations and goods facilities. Nevertheless a special train carrying the Directors was able to run on that deadline day, halting the spread of the broad gauge. Apart from the Great Western main line and the Oxford Worcester & Wolverhampton (most of which was laid to mixed gauge although no broad gauge train is known to have ventured west of Evesham) no broad gauge track penetrated the Midlands. Goods trains began running between Walsall and Dudley in March 1850 and passenger services began on 1st May, the day on which Bescot Curve opened. There were stations at Wednesbury, Great Bridge and Dudley Port. The last quarter mile of line was still incomplete, so there was a temporary station at Dudley for a few months, until a permanent station opened, adjoining the Oxford Worcester & Wolverhampton station. There was no rail connection between the two at first and, as described later, a feeling of separateness remained almost until the end of passenger services.

John Robinson McClean, Engineer

Having achieved the aim of halting the broad gauge, the unity of the South Staffs board soon collapsed, to be replaced by their own narrower interests. The independent faction proposed that the line should be leased, in order that they might be more certain of receiving a dividend. The others opposed this proposal, which was twice defeated when put to the shareholders. Soon afterwards, the LNWR and Midland did refuse to guarantee payment of a dividend, attitudes changed and the board was swiftly united again. They decided to lease the line to the company engineer, John Robinson McClean. There was no precedent for leasing a railway to an individual, so it triggered a special Act of Parliament. He had the lease for 21 years from July 1850, including track, locomotives and other rolling stock, for which he had to deposit the then enormous sum of £10,000 as a guarantee that he would carry out the contract to run the railway. Most board members thought, like so many other people in more recent times, that running a railway was easy and that they could do it better than the professionals. However, at the next meeting, when they attempted to issue McClean with instructions, he torpedoed them with one line - *"Gentlemen, I*

One of Francis Webb's 0-6-2 tank engines pauses at Brownhills, with a Lichfield - Walsall train, about 1908/09. The immaculate locomotive is in LNWR lined black, similar to the livery later adopted by British Railways. The guard's compartment in the middle of the leading six-wheel carriage is fitted with side windows. The man wearing gaiters obscures the view of the last vehicle in the rake, which has a different profile to the others. The gable end brickwork was laid with the ends (headers) alternating with the sides (stretchers) and the ornate lamp bracket shows signs of being a handy pigeon perch. This card was posted in Walsall in October 1910 and the message from Emily to her mother was "I arrived here safe. Am pleased to say I haven't jumped out of the frying pan into the fire".

(collection of Mrs.V.M.Beard)

A push-pull 'motor train' stands ready to be 'pushed' away from Wednesbury with a train for Walsall, about 1955. No.41223 is one of H.G.Ivatt's small 2-6-2 tank engines well suited to the task. *(Roger Carpenter)*

must remind you that I am now the boss".

McClean was a talented civil engineer whose contribution to his profession deserves to be more widely recognised. When appointed to the South Staffs in October 1846 he was already working for four other railway companies. Earlier, when apprenticed to a firm of civil engineers in London, he had prepared surveys and detailed drawings for the Victoria Embankment and the new Westminster Bridge. When new sewers were needed for the capital and the commissioners invited plans, his were the best of 116 submitted and the only ones which gave an estimate of the costs.

The South Staffs fixed his salary in unusual but practical terms, at the rate of £350 for every mile of line completed. Aged 33 when appointed, his growing earning power and huge appetite for work meant that he could easily afford the £10,000 guarantee when the line was leased to him in 1850. His many commitments sometimes clashed with one another. He was engineer of the Birmingham Wolverhampton & Dudley, yet in 1854 found himself having to oppose construction of a broad gauge branch of that line (already referred to) because of his work for the South Staffs. He was also embarrassed when one of his bridges on the BW&D main line, at Winson Green, collapsed the day after the inspector's train passed over it, causing the Great Western's Brunel to condemn five more of his bridges on the same line. This was a rare lapse.

During his work with the South Staffs, McClean became aware of the dreadful state of Walsall's water supply. The spectres of cholera and typhoid haunted the town at regular intervals. Further north, Lichfield's water was clean and pure. McClean secured the agreement of some powerful friends, including the Earl of Dudley, and the South Staffordshire Waterworks Company was formed in 1853. The idea was simple and brilliant - to supply Walsall and Dudley with Lichfield water (Stowe and Minster pools acting as reservoirs), burying the Dudley-made pipes alongside the railway. Parts of Walsall were connected by 1858 but it took fifteen years to complete the scheme. McClean was engineer but drew no salary. Because of this work it could be argued that, in his own way, he achieved as much for the general health of the people of Walsall as did Sister Dora.

By 1853 he was also busying himself with mining, completing a line serving two of the Marquis of Anglesey's pits on Cannock Chase, known then as the Hammerwich and Uxbridge pits, known more recently as Cannock Chase Colliery Nos. 1 & 2. The connection with the South Staffs line was at Anglesey Sidings, north of Brownhills. Money invested by McClean, the marquis and others helped to develop the Cannock Chase coalfield. The pits spawned the new communities of Chasetown and Chase Terrace, which were provided with schools, churches, a community centre and library by McClean. The opening of St.Anne's Free Church, Chasetown in 1865, was a high-profile occasion for a modest building in a mining village. McClean's friends from the British Association for the Advancement of Science travelled on a special train to Anglesey Sidings, from whence it was hauled along the branch to a special platform near the church. The locomotive was an 1856-built Beyer-Peacock 0-4-2 saddle tank, named "McClean", which saw a hundred years' service at the colliery.

Out On The Line

What sort of railway did McClean oversee? The company's chief clerk was George Potter Neele, a former head boy of Walsall's Queen Mary's Grammar School. He kept a record of events, a journal entitled "Railway Reminiscences". He noted that when faced with extra traffic the railway was unable to cope. The busiest day of the year was Whit Monday, when thousands

travelled to Lichfield for the Bower, a fair which had its origins in the Middle Ages. One year *we ventured on the very risky plan of using open wagons with planked seats"* - a practice that was by then illegal - the following year, excursionists were offered cattle trucks at very low fares, only to be mocked and mooed at by crowds of local urchins as the trains crawled into the City station.

Many stations were inadequate. Dudley was inconvenient and Wednesbury described as *"a low-lying, dingy, wooden structure reached through a mass of puddles"*. The busy sidings at Great Bridge were congested and on a gradient; so wagons were liable to smash through buffers and fall into the canal. As company headquarters, it was natural that Walsall should have the best station on the line, although there were only two platforms and two running lines until 1861. The tall redbrick buildings on Platform 1 remained in continuous railway use from 1849 until demolition in 1978. They were on Station Street but, as the station and the surrounding area developed, its centre of gravity shifted. Ever since the enlargement of 1883, the main entrance has been from Park Street.

By 1849 the South Staffs had a stud of 10 of its own locomotives, all numbered and named. Seven had the 2-2-2 wheel arrangement typical of the time. The oldest, No.2 "Walsall" was a Fairbairn design of 1842, No.7 "Bescot" was a Sharp of 1845 and all the others were new. By 1861 there were 29 locomotives - 11 types built by seven manufacturers! With such a small and very mixed bag, standardisation and efficient maintenance were impossible. The company had limited facilities, so heavy work was contracted out to Crewe, where these non-standard locos were detested. Many were named after locations on the line, such as "Pelsall", "Wednesbury", "Alrewas". Carriages and wagons were supplied by Henry Wright of Saltley Works.

In the early days the running of the South Staffs was primitive. The telegraph existed but was not properly exploited as it only linked the main stations. Trains were signalled on the time interval system, whereby a train was dispatched at a given time after the previous one. Should a train be late, a 'search party' was sent out. As Neele put it -

"In the case of passenger trains not arriving at central stations within twenty minutes of their due time, an engine would have to be sent out in search, the driver of the pilot engine having to exercise his best discretion on arriving at the spot where, from a goods train blocking the line or a train engine having failed, he came upon the belated passenger train".

In this the South Staffs was no better nor worse than most other lines at the time. Dudley was a particularly dangerous place because all South Staffs passenger trains had to work into and out of the same platform. With the lack of proper signalling, near misses were commonplace. There were two accidents, in October 1854 and May 1855. The second crash injured 40 passengers and the Board of Trade Inspector's report insisted that each engine into and out of the station should have a pilotman in the cab until the track layout was improved. The building of a joint station at Dudley, including track improvements and a physical link with the OWW, was sanctioned by an Act of July 1855.

There were two accidents between goods and passenger trains in 1853, at Great Bridge and Wednesbury. Both occurred when the offending train passed a signal at danger. A multiple collision between three freight trains, at the north end of Walsall station in December 1854, was caused when the second passed a signal at danger, running into the rear of the first train just before the third, travelling in the opposite direction, hit the wreckage of them both, killing its driver. As with the two earlier accidents, Sir Henry Tyler, responsible for the official inquiry, criticised the South Staffs and its drivers for routinely passing signals at

A Park Royal dmu, with silver roof, heads towards Hammerwich with the 4.31pm Burton-on-Trent - Lichfield - Walsall - Wolverhampton service on 25th July 1964, less than six months before the service was withdrawn. Park Royal of London was a major bus builder, but in 1957 twenty two-car diesel units were built for the London Midland Region at their Stockport works. Similar in design and appearance to the earlier Derby Lightweights, they had large saloons behind the driving cabs, with seating for 24 passengers (16 first class). Thus there were three windows between the cab and the first passenger door, not two. The trees are in the grounds of a pumping station of the South Staffordshire Waterworks and the train is about to pass under the main A461 Walsall - Lichfield road. This part of the line is still open for trains serving Charringtons Oil Terminal at Brownhills.   *(Michael Mensing)*

A special train for Lichfield Bower leaves Walsall in the capable hands of 0-6-0 goods loco No.44439 on Whit Monday, 29th May 1950. The stock is a rake of ex-Midland close coupled carriages. Bower Specials continued to run from Walsall until 1964.

(F.W.Shuttleworth)

danger. In the Walsall accident one driver had never been over the line before and another had been on duty for 26 hours. Tyler also found that at one place the signal was controlled by a 13-year-old girl!

"Derby" was an unfortunate choice for No.23, a Beyer-Peacock 0-4-2 goods loco, delivered new in 1855. By that year relations with the Midland Railway had deteriorated, following the appointment of James Allport as its General Manager. Through running ended, so exchange sidings and a small engine shed had to be built at Wichnor, together with a passenger station. This hostility only served to draw the South Staffs closer to the LNWR.

Expansion & Absorption

During the 1850s all the extensions to the South Staffs system were either built or sanctioned by Parliament. Every extension was also a link to the wider network. First was the half mile link with the LNWR's Stour Valley Line at Dudley Port, leaving the South Staffs at Sedgley Junction, which opened in January 1854. This difficult short curved line, with a gradient of 1:60, was worked by telegraph signalling almost from the beginning. During the twentieth century the one-and-a-quarter mile Dudley - Dudley Port (High Level) link was one of the most intensively worked push-pull services in the country and the 'Dudley Dasher' was familiar to most people in the town. It closed to passengers in 1964.

John Robinson McClean's lease of the South Staffs and his active interest in expanding mining activity in the Cannock area combined to promote the cause of a branch from Walsall to Cannock, which had been authorised in 1847 when the company was formed. These powers had lapsed, but a new Act was passed in 1854 and the line opened, together with a mineral branch to Norton Junction, on 1st February 1858. There were stations at Bloxwich, Wyrley & Church Bridge, and Cannock. A fourth station opened at Birchills two months later. The branch left the original main line by a new junction north of Walsall, at Ryecroft, a name familiar to generations of the town's railwaymen. The "Walsall Free Press" (6th February 1858) reported -

"On Monday last the Norton and Cannock branch of the South Staffs Railway was opened. It is calculated that this branch, by opening up a rich mineral district hitherto isolated for want of proper communication, will considerably augment the traffic on the main line."

As was the custom in most local papers throughout the country, a summary of the time-table was printed on the front page at least once a month. That for November 1858 is reproduced in full here, as it gives a clue to the flourishing state of the passenger service at the time, although trains to Lichfield and Cannock were few. The time-table does not discriminate between through and connecting services, but a change was always necessary for services via Dudley Port. Some times are duplicated, and some services run at very irregular intervals. Take, for example, the first five trains from Walsall to Birmingham ....

Walsall-Birmingham via Bescot
7.55am 9.0 11.0(fast) 11.15 12.30pm 1.5 1.45 3.25 5.40 6.10 7.15 9.15
Sundays 9.55am 10.25 2.55pm 5.30 8.25 9.20
Walsall-Birmingham via Dudley Port
6.40am 8.0 9.5 10.15 12.35pm 2.30 4.5 6.15 7.25 9.0
Sundays 6.30am 8.30 12.45pm 3.30 8.5 9.25
Walsall-Wolverhampton via Bescot
8.25am 9.45 11.15 11.55 1.5pm 2.40 5.10 5.40 7.15 9.15 10.45
Sundays 8.50am 1.20pm 6.5 10.45

Walsall-Wolverhampton via Dudley Port
8.0am 9.5 10.15 12.35pm 2.30 4.5 6.15 7.25 9.0
Sundays 8.35am 12.45pm 3.30 8.5 9.25
Walsall-Dudley
6.40am 8.0 9.5 10.15 12.35pm 2.30 4.5 6.15 7.25 9.0 11.10
Sundays 6.30am 8.35 9.55 12.45pm 3.30 6.35 8.50 9.25
Walsall-Lichfield
8.15am 10.10 11.45 4.5pm 4.30(SO, to Brownhills only) 7.20 9.45 (SO)
Sundays 7.45am 9.50 3.30pm 6.30
Walsall-Cannock
7.30am 10.15 4.15pm 7.30 10.0 (SO)
Sundays 10.0am 3.45pm 6.45

The extension from Cannock to Rugeley was promoted by a separate company, as described in the next chapter. An Act of July 1855 granted permission for construction of the Princes End and Darlaston loop lines as well as Leighswood Siding and the Wyrley goods line. The loops both opened in September 1863, by which time the South Staffs was under LNWR control. The Darlaston Loop (see Chapter 5) lost its passenger trains in 1887 but remained busy with freight traffic until the 1960s. The Princes End Loop closed to passengers as a wartime economy in January 1916, but it continued in use for regular freight and diverted passenger trains until closure in 1981. A short mixed gauge spur to the South Staffs was provided by the Great Western, at Wednesbury, in June 1859. Busy exchange sidings were later established here.

Before the end of the prosperous 1850s it was apparent that McClean's lease of the railway was becoming unworkable. Board members with LNWR interest applied increasing pressure - a takeover bid. In 1858 it was agreed that the lease be transferred to the LNWR, which would also buy the 29 locomotives. McClean would be compensated for the unexpired part of his lease, set to run until 1871. There was a deal of acrimonious haggling, with claims, counter claims and appeals for arbitration, before a sum was agreed. The figure was £110,099, which made an already wealthy man stupendously rich. It represented the income he could have expected from the prosperous South Staffs had traffic remained buoyant and had he remained until 1871. The lease was transferred to the LNWR on 1st February 1861, which finally absorbed the line in July 1867.

Having charge of the lease, the LNWR soon attempted to re-establish running rights to Derby via Wichnor Junction. The first train north, with Neele on the footplate, found the line blocked -

"Arriving at Wichnor Junction I was surprised to see a large number of platelayers, about two or three engines in steam, and a saloon carriage in the siding. One of the engines with steam up had attached to its tender the V crossing of the junction over which we had to pass to get to Burton."

The superintendent of the Midland, who had spent the night in the saloon, refused to allow the LNW train to pass -

"On asking Mr.Needham for what purpose the force of Midland men was requisitioned, he told me that it was reported that the London and North-Western were coming down with a body of 300 men and three engines intending to force their way into Burton, and that it had been determined to resist."

By the afternoon of the same day the Midland relented, the platelayers melted away and the LNWR train, somewhat provocatively, *"made a triumphal journey towards Burton, the engine-driver taking the opportunity of sounding noisy and repeated cock crows on his steam whistle."* From then until closure to passengers in 1965, some trains provided a through service between Walsall, Burton and Derby via Lichfield.

Cannock station, looking north, about 1900, with what appears to be a Webb coal engine. The reason for this posed photograph is now a mystery.   *(courtesy of Staffordshire Library Services, Cannock Library)*

Photographs of Bloxwich station are rare. This shot, taken in 1962, shows a Ryecroft based Park Royal dmu entering the station with a Rugley Trent Valley - Birmingham train.   *(Nick Sanders)*

One of Ryecroft's pool of Fowler 2-6-2 tank engines, in charge of a Walsall-Rugeley train, leaves the Black Country behind. It is seen here north of Bloxwich, just past Essington distant signal, on a fine summer evening in 1934. The clear light highlights the lineside fencing, built to the LNWR's standard pattern.

(Frank Ash)

Everything In Duplicate

In the beginning there had been problems at Dudley because the South Staffs and Oxford Worcester & Wolverhampton stations were near to, but separate from, each other. Both stations were little more than sheds and little attempt was made to co-ordinate time-tables. Suggestions for a joint station always foundered in bickering and petty rivalry. In due course the travelling public was relieved of this burden when the South Staffs station burnt down and a joint station was constructed. In the best tradition of rival companies compelled to work together, there were two of everything, especially two different ways of doing things. This persisted until the formation of British Railways in 1948. Kenneth Tibbetts, who later became a Methodist minister, began three years' work as a junior clerk at Dudley, for the LMS, in February 1938. He wrote an article for "The Blackcountryman" magazine (autumn 1993), describing his work, including the duplication of virtually everything at this LMS & GWR joint station. On a normal weekday there were about 140 train departures between 05.00 and 23.30. The Dudley Dasher auto train to Dudley Port, with about 50 movements, was the the most intensive service. There were about 16 trains to Walsall, 20 on the Great Western to Birmingham, plus services to Wolverhampton Low Level, Stourbridge Junction, not forgetting the 'Bumble Hole' line to Old Hill. There were nine clerks, all of whom had to be familiar with both companies' different ways of doing things. Faced with the morning rush hour, and the issuing of over 200 tickets, company loyalties buckled under pressure and tickets for all lines were sold by both companies' clerks from both the GWR and LMS ticket windows. At quiet times, with just one clerk on duty, if he appeared at the GWR window and the passenger wanted a ticket for an LMS station, they were told to 'go to the other window', only to find the same clerk's face appear. Clerks had to calculate and pay out wages for platform, yard and signal box staff - with a different system for each company. Cash from ticket sales was also processed differently, as described by Kenneth -

"The two different accounting systems involved different ways of remitting the takings. Each weekday one of the senior clerks went to a bank in the town to pay in the previous day's LMS receipts, but the GW cash was sent direct to the District Cashier in Worcester. For this purpose a travelling safe was conveyed in the guard's van of the 8.49 train every morning, and at each station a padlocked leather pounch containing the previous day's cash was inserted. the (Dudley) pouch was prepared by the chief clerk on the previous afternoon and placed in the office safe. Then, for greater security, it was transferred each night to a safe provided specially for this purpose in the South Signal Box at the end of the GW platform."

There were two goods stations, the Great Western one in the station drive on the castle side of the station, the LMS one fronting Tipton Road. There were, of course, exchange sidings. The mere transfer of goods traffic between the two railways at

God's Wonderful Railway meets the Premier Line at Dudley, looking north, about 1959. It is obvious, from the pannier tank loco, the signalling and the platform seat, that the Great Western part of the station is in the left foreground. The large number of people in summer dress on the far platform may well be on their way home after an excursion to the zoo. Beyond the station the South Staffs line curves under the Tipton Road bridge, seen above the footbridge.   *(Roger Carpenter)*

A 4-6-0 Ivatt 'Flying Pig', No.43022 on the turntable at Bescot, having worked an excursion to Dudley Zoo from Nuneaton. The turntable was activated by the loco's vacuum pipe.
(Ray Churchill)

A lightly loaded Park Royal diesel multiple unit leaves Dudley Port with the 4.14pm from Dudley to Walsall on 2nd May 1964. This service was withdrawn on 4th July of that year. A train of early steel-bodied corridor stock in maroon livery is on the Stour Valley main line. Back garden pigeon lofts, some of which are striped as here, remain a feature of much of the Black Country. *(Michael Mensing)*

Dudley, which generated not a penny for either the GWR or LMS, provided enough paperwork to keep two clerks from the Railway Clearing House fully employed in their own office in the GW part of the station.

Only ghosts remain at the derelict site of Dudley joint station, as the weeds increase, the track blackens with rust and at least one road sign continues to point the way to the Freightliner depot. Numbered among the ghosts there must be countless thousands of Irish pigs, which arrived at Palethorpe's sidings on their final journey, to emerge from the factory as sausages, pork pies, etc. Palethorpe's red-liveried refrigerated vans were familiar sights throughout the Midlands. The sidings were on the east side of the line, just north of Sedgeley Junction, where the short loop line began its climb to Dudley Port High Level. Sedgley itself is west of Bilston, the junction was named after the nearest road, Sedgley Road East, picking up an extra 'e' along the way. Sedgeley Junction box was busy, with movements to Palethorpe's and the industrial sidings for Coneygre and Babcock & Wilcox, as well as the comings and going of the Dasher, other local trains, heavy freights between South Wales and Bescot and - in summer - excursions to the zoo, where the stock was stabled in carriage sidings controlled by this box. Standard bell codes had special variations, so that the harassed signalman could distinguish the Dasher and other movements to and from the high level line.

The duplication at Dudley and many other places was an interesting slice of railway history, but a huge waste of money and resources. As today's privatised network fragments, and unnecessary rivalries and duplications reappear within the industry, the wheel is turning full circle as the lessons of past mistakes seem not to have been learnt.

Fuel For Thought

Recent fortunes of the South Staffs line have been very mixed, as a look at the whole route will confirm. Wichnor to Lichfield Trent Valley is open for freight, including some Merry Go Round (mgr) coal workings between Rugeley Power Station and the East Midlands; Lichfield Trent Valley to City is the northern end of the electrified Birmingham Cross City Line; Lichfield City to Anglesey Sidings sees a maximum of three trains per week to Charringtons Fuels; Anglesey Sidings to Ryecroft was closed on 19th March 1984, the track has been lifted and the trackbed is safeguarded for the moment; Ryecroft to Walsall is open for freight and the diesel passenger service to Hednesford; Walsall to Pleck Junction is part of the electric line to Bescot and Birmingham; south of Pleck Junction the track gently rusts, urgently awaiting a decision on its future.

Charrington's Fuel Distribution Depot is situated at Anglesey Sidings, just north of Brownhills. It is the only reason for the continued existence of the section of line from Lichfield City, reduced to single track and served by up to three trains per week, according to seasonal demand. The train normally runs on Tuesdays, Thursdays and/or Saturdays. Having gained permission to visit the site, I arrived very early one clear Saturday morning in May 1996, to witness its arrival, always scheduled for 04.53. The train description number is 6M65, leaving Lindsey Oil Refinery, Immingham at 01.30, travelling south from Burton via Wichnor to Lichfield City. A ladder crossing south of the station leads onto the single track. Two colour light signals each control access to and from the branch. They are operated from the Aston Signalling Centre at Duddeston, which controls the northern part of the Cross City Line, from Aston to Lichfield

26

31 126 and 31 199 nearing Fosseway Crossing with a train for Charrington's Fuels on 22nd March 1990. The three spires belong to Lichfield Cathedral.
(G. Hopkinson)

Trent Valley. Having worked along the branch, just over four miles long with a line speed limit of 20mph, the train reaches the ground frame which gives access to the run-round loop and Charrington's two sidings. The driver contacts Aston Signalling Centre from the trackside phone, the signaller releases the frame and shunting movements can begin. The locomotive (60 070 "John Lauden McAdam" on my visit) runs round its train and propels the tankers, at less than walking pace, past the depot's boundary gates and into the two sidings. The space between the sidings is occupied by three pipes, the middle one of which is connected to the gas oil storage tank. The others, which are lagged and steam heated, are for fuel oil.

The depot storage tanks have a total storage capacity of 12.5 million litres. This consists of heavy, medium and light fuel oil (for industrial use), gas oil (domestic heating), derv and kerosene. All the heavy and medium fuel oil, and more than half the gas oil, is brought in by rail, about 60% of the total. Charrington's is the largest independent fuel distributor in the UK, with 21 depots throughout the country, of which this is the largest. Only two others are served by rail, at Derby and Cambridge. Onward delivery by road tanker from Brownhills covers an area bounded by Stoke-on Trent, Market Harborough, Hereford and the Welsh border. The vital contribution rail makes is put into context when looking at the capacity of a single train - more than one million litres - fifty times greater than the 20,000 litres for a road tanker.

On the day of my visit the train consisted of 28 heavy fuel tankers (868,000 litres) and 7 gas oil tankers (255,500 litres). Prior to arrival the pipe heating had been switched on, causing much of the site to be enveloped in steam. Charringtons own the

tankers, most of which were built at Doncaster in the 1960s, and although most are lagged, a few are not, hence the heating. The fuel had been loaded at Immingham twenty-four hours earlier. In cold weather, and especially in unlagged tanks, the heavy oil can soon have the consistency of tar. One biting east coast Saturday in the winter of 1996 the train could not leave Immingham, due to the heavy falling snow. On rare occasions at Brownhills it has not proved possible to offload the fuel on the same day, causing the tankers to be left 'on steam' overnight. A hose connects each tanker to the discharge pipe and it normally takes about six hours to offload a whole train. The fuel oil storage tanks are lagged and they each have a reservoir of steam-heated water at their base.

In the past the trains have been hauled by Class 20s or 31s working in pairs, more recently by Class 37 or 47 locos. Normal haulage today is by a Class 60, with occasional use of a Class 56. The empty tanks are due to leave, as train 7E71, at 14.35, with an Immingham arrival at 18.15. On the journey south there is a driver change at Nottingham. A second man is taken on board at Lichfield, for shunting duties at Brownhills. Soon after arrival they are collected by road and taken to Bescot, to complete their shift by working another train north. The new crew is delivered from Bescot just before departure, the railman travels to Lichfield and the driver takes the train as far as Nottingham before working back to Bescot on other duties.

At a time when part of the South Staffs has been lifted, and the section south of Pleck Junction lies rusting, it is encouraging that Charringtons remain keen to work with the rail authorities, and see themselves as having a long term rail-served future at Brownhills.

(The Cannock Mineral Railway : Coal : A Modern Survivor)

The Web of Lines Around Cannock

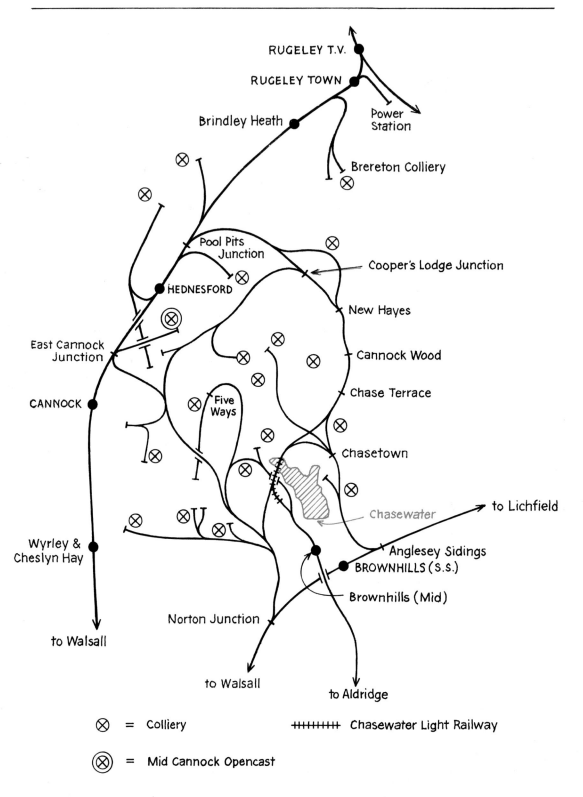

RUGELEY T.V.

RUGELEY TOWN

Brindley Heath

Power Station

Brereton Colliery

Pool Pits Junction

Cooper's Lodge Junction

HEDNESFORD

New Hayes

Cannock Wood

East Cannock Junction

Chase Terrace

CANNOCK

Five Ways

Chasetown

Chasewater

to Lichfield

Wyrley & Cheslyn Hay

Anglesey Sidings
BROWNHILLS (S.S.)

Brownhills (Mid)

Norton Junction

to Walsall

to Walsall

to Aldridge

⊗ = Colliery   ++++++++ Chasewater Light Railway

⊗ = Mid Cannock Opencast

The Cannock Mineral Railway

It took thirteen years before the idea of a railway linking Cannock with Rugeley Trent Valley became a reality. The first development can only be described as a farce, in which the chief player was George Remington, spectacularly out of his depth. This gentleman, along with Sir John Rennie, was appointed Engineer of the Derbyshire Staffordshire & Worcestershire Junction Railway (beware of small companies with inflated titles) which, at the same time as the South Staffs was being proposed, was planning its own line from Dudley through Walsall and Cannock to a junction with the North Staffs at Uttoxeter. Remington appeared before a Parliamentary Committee in 1846 to put the case for the line. Not content merely to shoot himself in the foot, he chose to riddle himself with bullets. He admitted that he had never laid a line through such a thinly populated district. He did not know if the people of either the Black Country or the Potteries felt the need for a rail link, even though passenger traffic was seen as the greatest source of revenue, especially at Wednesbury. Regarding traffic potential around Cannock Chase, he remarked that it was "by no means more unpopulated" than the bleak wastes of Chat Moss on the Liverpool & Manchester. The bill for this railway was rejected by the Lords. The company modified its ambitions, though not yet its title, and in the next session of Parliament presented a bill for an 18 mile line linking Cannock with Uttoxeter via Rugeley. This became an Act on 2nd July 1847, a week before the Act for the South Staffordshire Railway, which included provision for a line from Walsall to Cannock. Nothing happened at first, and powers to build these lines lapsed.

The South Staffs renewed powers for its Cannock branch in 1854 and the line opened four years later. In 1855 the Derbyshire etc.etc.Railway came down to earth and changed its name to the Cannock Mineral Railway (CMR). Although there was a passenger service from the beginning, the new title recognised the overriding importance of freight. The line to Uttoxeter was to be abandoned, and the entire route consisted of a short but vital link between Cannock and Rugeley Trent Valley. Plans for a separate station at Cannock were abandoned in favour of sharing the South Staffs premises. An Act for the railway in this form was passed in August 1855. It contained provision (surprise!) for the LNWR to lease the line, which it did from the opening, despite a bungled attempt by the North Staffs and CMR to form an alliance.

The CMR was engineered by Thomas Brassey and opened on 7th November 1859. Much of the seven mile line crosses the Chase and its most obvious physical feature is the high embankment on the approach to Rugeley. At first the only intermediate station was Hednesford. A bridge carrying what is now Market Street over the line, at the station, was not built until 1875. A very early photograph shows a level crossing and a signal, with arms for each direction on the post, and lights lower down. The station appears to be in the middle of nowhere, with Cannock Chase stretching to the horizon beyond the small posed group on the short platform. The 38-lever signal box at Hednesford is one of the oldest LNWR boxes still in use, dating from 1877.

In the early days, the isolated nature of the line made it easy for some railwaymen to supplement their income, as told by Neele in his "Railway Reminiscences" -

"Mysterious robberies of goods were constantly taking place ...... The guard, fireman and driver of the night goods train systematically stopped opposite the wildest part of the chase, rifled the most promising truck and hid the spoils in a regular smugglers cave they had constructed; the absence of any system of signalling from section to section removed any means of

Hednesford station, looking north, before 1875.

(Author's collection)

recording undue delays .... a lengthy term of imprisonment was the sequel to this performance."

Eventually there were two more intermediate stations on the line. Rugeley Town opened in June 1870, on the embankment above Horsefair. It was a neat and typical LNWR wayside station, with wooden platforms and small chalet buildings. There followed almost fifty years of confusion. The Trent Valley station continued to be known simply as 'Rugeley' for many years on the station nameboards. The LNWR printed it as 'Rugeley (Trent Valley)' in the Walsall line time-table, but just 'Rugeley' in the Trent Valley line table. Many local people pronounce their town Rudgeley (rhyming with 'fudge') and Bradshaw's Railway Guide showed Rugeley Trent Valley as Rudgeley Junction. It took until 1917 before both stations were consistent in their spellings and titles in all publicity.

As the Second World War loomed, an RAF site was developed at Brindley Heath. The station here was opened for air force traffic on 3rd August 1939, for public use on 26th August and for parcels in November. It closed in 1959.

Coal

The Cannock Mineral Railway, leased by the LNWR from the day it opened, was formally absorbed in July 1869. Ever since it opened it has formed part of the Rugeley - Cannock - Walsall artery by which coal has left Cannock Chase. For the remainder of the nineteenth century, the coalfield spawned a network of mineral lines, plus optimistic ideas for lines that were never built. Near Rugeley, the important branch to Brereton Colliery opened in 1875. The 20-lever LNWR signal box at Brereton Sidings, still in use, dates from 1908. The branch into Rugeley Power Station opened in 1957. Among the lines not built were the Cannock Chase & Wolverhampton Railway, authorised in 1864 to build a line connecting Cannock with Wolverhampton via Burntwood. The Wolverhampton end was to connect with the Great Western at Cannock Road Junction and an extension to Hednesford was authorised in 1866. This attempt by the GWR to invade alien territory came to nothing. There were also plans for a Cannock & Wolverhampton Light Railway, which were being seriously considered as late as 1926.

The principal lines crossing the coalfield were a modified amalgam of earlier schemes, including parts of the Cannock Chase & Wolverhampton. Together with sections of a planned Cannock Chase Extension Railway, it formed a link between the Cannock main line at East Cannock Junction, and the South Staffs line at Norton Junction. The Marquis of Anglesey's line through Chasetown, engineered by John Robinson McClean and referred to in Chapter Two, joined forces with other lines to form another link between the Cannock and South Staffs lines, between Pool Pits and Anglesey junctions. A whole network of minor lines provided the infill. Any railway map showing the coalfield lines is certainly complex and likely to be inaccurate. So many small lines, spurs, sidings etc. were built and - in some instances - rapidly disappeared or changed with the fortunes of the pits they served. None was widely known outside the coalfield because they carried no public passenger service, although trains were provided to carry miners to and from work in an assortment of vintage rolling stock. There was, briefly, a public passenger service of sorts. The LNWR stabled three motor buses near the station at Brownhills and began a service to Hednesford, via Chase Terrace, in October 1912. It ended abruptly when the vehicles were requisitioned by the army shortly after the outbreak of war in August 1914.

By 1879 the Midland Railway had opened its own route between Birmingham, Walsall and Wolverhampton. This gave it easier access to LNWR territory, including Walsall. The Birmingham - Walsall section went through Sutton Park, giving this part of the line its name. The Midland also wanted direct access to the coalfield and to this end an important branch left the Sutton Park line at Aldridge. It reached the coalfield via Walsall Wood and Brownhills. It connected with the Cannock Chase & Wolverhampton near Chasewater, a reservoir often known as Norton Pool until recent years. The line opened to goods in November 1882. It served several large collieries and was partly double track. Two years later, almost as an afterthought, a passenger service was provided on the four mile section between Aldridge and Brownhills, with an intermediate station at Walsall Wood. The station at Brownhills, known as Brownhills Watling Street after 1924, was about a mile from the town and almost as far from the LNW station. Aldridge - Brownhills was hardly a key commuter corridor and trains were always few. Three weekday trains each way in 1910 (five on Saturdays) had shrunk to two each way, six days a week by 1929. The service ceased in March 1930.

Goods traffic continued only for as long as this part of the coalfield prospered. Gradually output dwindled, pits were

A Super D approaches East Cannock Junction from Hednesford with a train of coal for Norton Junction via the Leacroft and Norton branch, 1956.   *(Maurice Newman)*

exhausted, and the line closed in 1962. About a mile was retained at the Aldridge end and used for stabling some of the overhead electrification rolling stock when the main lines in the area were being energised. It served this purpose until at least 1966.

At Walsall Wood, a hump and blue brick parapets show where the road to Lichfield once passed over the line. The station area has been landscaped and given over to a playground. However, part of the branch is still intact.

Two views of the last train at Brownhills Watling Street. Johnson 0-6-0 No. 3277 prepares to leave with the 4.20pm (SO) to Aldridge on 29th March 1930. The smaller carriage has six-wheel bogies. *(Bill Mayo collection)*

The Leighswood Branch

A mineral branch, known as Leighswood Siding, opened from Pelsall (Heath End Sidings) to Leighswood Colliery in 1878. Long after the colliery closed, the line remained open to serve the Atlas Brickworks and Aldridge Brick & Tile Works. Ex-Midland loco 58157 is seen crossing the canal on the way to the brickworks, after which it would propel its stock to the tile works (below). There was a connection with the Aldridge-Brownhills line by means of an Annetts Key token. Photographs of the Leighswood branch are very rare. These date from 8th September 1953.   *(F.W.Shuttleworth)*

A Cannock Miners' Train

A miners train to Hednesford from Rawnsley, 15th May 1952. No.50705, normally shedded at Warrington, was on loan to the NCB. The six-wheeled stock once belonged to the Great Eastern, Maryport & Carlisle and Furness Railways. *(F.W.Shuttleworth)*

Having arrived at Pool Pits Junction, Hednesford, the miners disembark. *(F.W.Shuttleworth)*

A Modern Survivor

Chasewater is a reservoir formed when a valley was dammed in the early days of the coalfield. Water pumped out of the mines was stored here and the reservoir acted as a header tank to supply the local canals and keep them full. The Chasewater Light Railway consists of the northern tip of the Midland line from Aldridge and a section of the Cannock Chase & Wolverhampton. It began operating in 1970 and has expanded slowly until there is now one and a quarter miles of line on the northern shore of the reservoir. There are plans to lay more line along the trackbed towards Burntwood. In keeping with the spirit of the coalfield lines, the motive power is provided entirely by industrial locomotives.

There is a 0-4-0 saddle tank, No.2780 "Asbestos", built by Hawthorn Leslie of Newcastle in 1909. It worked the internal railway belonging to Turner Asbestos, Manchester, and was donated to the Chasewater line in 1972, when it hauled the first steam passenger trains on the line. The oldest working loco is No.2937 0-4-0 saddle tank "Sir Alfred Paget", built by Neilson of Glasgow in 1882. Until 1950 it worked at Glenboig Colliery, near Coatbridge, when it was transferred to Gartsherrie Iron Works. It was acquired by Chasewater in 1968, before any part of the line was operational. The newest and most unusual steam loco was built in 1957 by the Sentinel Steam Wagon & Carriage Co. of Shrewsbury. This vertical boilered loco worked at Pleck Gasworks for just eleven years. Several such locos are preserved, but very few lines operate them on a regular basis. Chasewater does, which is one reason why it is so popular among enthusiasts. At present the railway has a stock of 10 steam and 6 diesel industrial locos, some awaiting restoration.

There are about 16 wagons and vans, three of which definitely belonged to local colliery lines - a brake van and two 'four-plank' 5-ton coal wagons. There are some hidden gems amongst the coaching stock. The greatest rarity is a six-wheeled five-compartment carriage, built in 1875, the last survivor from the Maryport & Carlisle Railway. It sits alongside a Manchester Sheffield & Lincoln six-wheeled brake dating from 1898. Both have wooden centred so-called Maunsell wheels. Like the Maryport & Carlisle carriage, an 1885 Midland Railway four-wheeled brake van once helped transport men across the coalfield, the nearest thing these lines ever had to a passenger service. A considerable amount of time, money and effort will have to be spent before any of these vehicles can carry fare paying passengers again. A long term hope must lie with the extension of the railway to a centre of population, such as Chasetown. The present passenger stock consists of Class 116 and 117 dmus, which are steam hauled.

Like most preserved lines, the Chasewater Light Railway is run by enthusiastic volunteers. What makes it unusual is the way it tries to capture the atmosphere of the industrial lines that were once so common throughout the country. The stock of locos includes ones that once worked in collieries, steelworks, gasworks, Cadbury's at Bournville and Bass at Burton. As well as promoting what is often a neglected area of railway history, a line such as the Chasewater is a reminder of rail's vital role, without which the industries of this country would not have been able to function.

The Chasewater Light Railway has preserved a section of mineral line north of Brownhills, one of many that used to criss-cross the South Staffordshire coalfield. Something of the atmosphere of its earlier existence is apparent on 'Gricer's Day', 9th October 1977. The two sturdy little four-wheel tank engines, all power and no frills, are "Alfred Paget" (left) and "Invicta". Such locos were once busy in their hundreds on mineral lines and within factory, colliery and dockside sites throughout the country.   (D.Beech)

A scene at Hednesford LNWR exchange sidings, about 1930. The 0-6-0 saddle tank, No.2 "Anglesey", belongs to Cannock & Rugeley Collieries, as do the wooden-sided 10 ton trucks, each full of 'noted house coal'. The head shunter is distinguished his superior headgear; the loco is immaculate. *(Roger Carpenter collection)*

Sentinel steam shunter at Walsall Gas Works, shortly after delivery from its Shrewsbury makers in 1957. Defined as a 4wVBT (four-wheel vertical boiler tank) this loco now runs on the Chasewater Light Railway. *(Roger Carpenter)*

CHAPTER FOUR : A GREAT WAY ROUND
The Midland Route; Birmingham - Walsall - Wolverhampton

(The Wolverhampton & Walsall Railway : The Sutton Park Line :
Their Finest Hour : More Recent History)

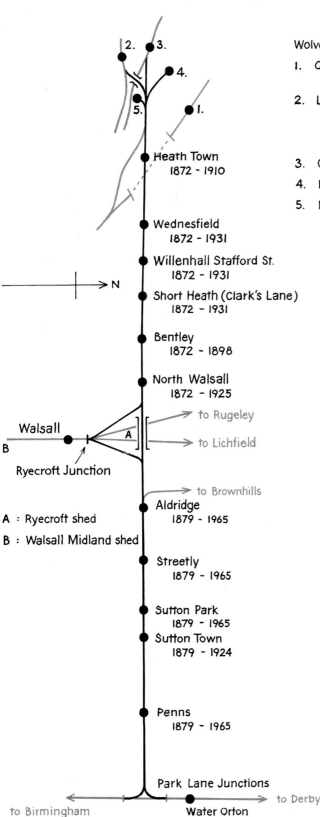

Wolverhampton Stations –

1. Grand Junction Station
   (later 'Wednesfield Heath')

2. L N W R Station –
   Known as 'Queen Street',
   then 'High Level',
   now plain 'Wolverhampton'

3. Great Western 'Low Level' Station

4. Midland Goods Station

5. Midland Canal Depot

The Wolverhampton & Walsall Railway

The phrase 'Great Way Round' suggests the Great Western Railway before it shortened many of its main lines by building 'cut-offs' early in the twentieth century. Here it refers to the Midland and its route between Birmingham and Wolverhampton via Walsall, which was built in two stages.

By the 1860s Wolverhampton and Walsall were the two largest towns in Staffordshire, yet there was still no direct rail link between them. The change of train necessary at Bescot meant that it was often as quick to travel by road coach, as the train took 45 minutes. The buildings at Bescot were described in a letter to the "Willenhall Magazine", signed by 'Corn Dealer', as *a miserable wooden shed, not fit to house cattle, and here passengers of every description, including poor people thinly clad, are compelled to wait perhaps 15 minutes on dark winter evenings, without fire or light".* After 1863 it was possible to travel in a through train via Princes End, though this was hardly direct. The LNWR could not be persuaded to build a direct line, despite the best efforts, over a two year period, of the Earl of Lichfield, so two Wolverhampton solicitors, H.H.Fowler and H.E.Underhill, gathered support from the earl, and local industrialists, for an independent railway. The Act for the Wolverhampton & Walsall Railway (W&W) was passed in 1865. Although some influential citizens of Wolverhampton were the driving force behind the line's creation, to the people of Walsall at the time W&W stood for Walsall & Wolverhampton Railway. The line was to run via Short Heath and Willenhall, connecting with the Great Western at Wolverhampton and the South Staffs line at Ryecroft. Original plans had been for an independent station in Walsall, 17 feet above the level of Park Street. Although it would have been inconvenient, it was welcomed by the town's Improvement Commissioners because it would have swept away the disease-ridden slums around Marsh Lane.

A rare photograph of the interior of the ex-Midland Railway signal box at Willenhall Stafford Street, taken in July 1960. It was fitted with a standard Midland tumbler signal frame, with slots for the levers at 6 inch intervals. Midland levers had catch handles to the rear, LNWR levers had stirrup handles at the front. These needed to be pulled to activate the lever but if the lever was locked the catch handle could not be released, thus preventing strain on the mechanism. (In contrast, catch handles on standard Great Western levers could be released even when the lever was locked). *(Mick Shaw)*

However, the increasing influence of the LNWR, which wanted to bring the line under its own control and into its own stations at Walsall and Wolverhampton, won the day. An 1866 amendment transferred the connection at Wolverhampton from the GW to the LNWR line, although in the event connecting lines were built into both Wolverhampton stations, and the Midland and GWR were to have running rights over the W&W. The thwarted wish for a separate station at Walsall was understandable. The LNWR structure was becoming overcrowded both with trains and people, yet the company failed to provide adequate waiting rooms or even a footbridge. A direct LNWR route to Wolverhampton, via a new spur from Pleck to James Bridge junctions, did not open until 1881 and improvements to Walsall station were not forthcoming until 1883.

Meanwhile, John Addison was appointed Engineer of the W&W and, after withdrawal of the original contractor - Waring Brothers - the contract was taken up by Thomas Brassey. This railway proved to be his last work as he died before it was completed. Work began in 1867 and proceeded very slowly. The cost of land purchase, at £110,000, was four times the estimate; extra work was required to secure the line against subsidence from old uncharted mine workings, and in 1869 Thomas Brassey refused to continue unless he was paid.

The W&W, which had its head office in Darlington Street, Wolverhampton, was opened on 1st November 1872, with stations at North Walsall, Bentley, Short Heath (Clark's Lane), Willenhall Market Place (renamed Stafford St. in 1924), Wednesfield and Heath Town. As the following day's "Walsall Observer" noted, rather oddly, *"Yesterday the new line of railway was formally opened for the transmission of passengers"*. There were eight trains from Walsall, nine in return, with three on Sundays. During its first year the line was used by over 470,000

passengers and generated 14,783 tons of general goods and mineral traffic. It was absorbed by the LNWR in 1875 and sold to the Midland a year later, which increased the number of trains to 28 each way. From 1909 both companies used each others routes between Walsall and Wolverhampton, both conveniently avoiding the need for their Birmingham-Walsall-Wolverhampton local trains to reverse at Walsall.

Despite the improved service, there was a steady decline in the number of passengers. Bentley closed in 1898 due to tramway competition, Heath Town followed in 1910. The busiest station, Willenhall, saw 149,000 passengers in 1877, 92,000 in 1892, 80,000 in 1907 and only 34,000 in 1922, by which time the number of daily trains was down to seven in each direction. The service was withdrawn on 5th January 1931 but the line remained open for freight, even after it was cut in two!

It was severed at Birchills in September 1964 to allow for construction of the M6. A short middle section was lifted and the western end mothballed. Birchills coal fired power station had opened in 1949, having cost £12 million. Each of its six 240' high cooling towers weighed 2,500 tons. At first coal was supplied by rail and canal and the internal sidings were worked by two Ruston & Hornsby 0-4-0 diesel shunters. After 1964 all rail deliveries were via Ryecroft, up to five 40-wagon trains per day until 1977, over half Birchills' needs of 450,000 tons per annum. By then the power station was seen as outmoded and too expensive to upgrade - the cooling water could only be provided by the adjacent canal - and consumption of coal fell to 190,000 tons in 1979. Only 25% of this was delivered by rail, uneconomic for both the CEGB and BR. The line closed in May 1980 followed by the power station in 1982. Demolition was completed in 1985 and the site given over to open cast.

The western section of the W&W was reopened in 1970 to serve Tube Investments Weldless Ltd., of Wednesfield, which received steel from Round Oak via a new siding, complete with an overhead magnetic crane. Normally there were two trains per week, usually 10 flat wagons of steel bars, with a Class 25 loco in charge. Nearby, Ductile Steel also had its own siding, overhead crane and diesel shunter. Deliveries by rail to both these companies ceased in 1981 and the last section of the Wolverhampton & Walsall Railway was closed and lifted soon afterwards.

Probably the last revenue earning train along the Wolverhampton & Walsall line, 17th March 1981. Deliveries to Ductile Steel, Wednesfield, were by a train from Scunthorpe, which was stabled overnight in Bescot yard. The journey was completed when the train, having arrived at Heath Town Junction, was drawn forward by a Class 08 diesel shunter. On this occasion the loco was 08 585 and, contrary to usual practice, the train locos - 20 188 and 20 186 - were also worked along the line, 'dead'. *(Philip Barnard)*

Aldridge in 1908, with Midland Railway local trains bound for Birmingham (right) and Wolverhampton via Walsall. The large goods shed it situated on the Brownhills branch. The station had not yet been supplied with standard Midland boundary fencing, where the timbers were set at 45 degrees.

(Walsall Local History Centre)

The Sutton Park Line

When the W&W was nearing completion, an Act was passed in August 1872, for a Walsall Wolverhampton & Midland Junction Railway (absorbed by the Midland in 1874), more easily known as the Sutton Park line. It was to join the three other lines at Ryecroft and have a direct connection with the W&W by means of an avoiding line just to the north. It would connect with the Birmingham-Derby main line by means of a trangular junction south of Water Orton. There was much opposition in Sutton Coldfield when the inhabitants realised that the railway was to cross Sutton Park, 2,400 acres of open unspoilt land, given to the town by Bishop Vesey in 1528. The promoters pointed out that the new line would supply Sutton with cheap coal from the Nottinghamshire coalfield, courtesy of the Midland Railway. The necessary two mile strip of land through the park was bought for £6,500. Some inhabitants remained unhappy at the thought of a railway scarring their park, despite the prospect of cheaper coal. It was felt necessary to provide a clause in the Act which would camouflage the trains passing through Sutton Park -

"The said Warden & Society" (Sutton's equivalent of Mayor and Corporation) *"may at any time and at their expense plant and cultivate shrubs on the embankments of the Railway within the Park of Sutton Coldfield, Provided always that the cultivation of such shrubs shall not interfere with the working of the Railway."*

Even before the line was sanctioned by Parliament, some preliminary surveying at Rushall caused excitement in the "Walsall Free Press" (4th November 1871), which recommended that the promoters should have a separate station in Walsall, thus avoiding any connection with the LNWR, whose station was 'a disgrace to the town'.

The railway had to bear the expense of constructing an aqueduct for the Daw End Branch Canal, which was to cross the line near the west end of Blue Hole Cutting, between Aldridge and Ryecroft.

As with so many railways and other large civil engineering projects, the actual construction costs for the Sutton Park line (£400,000), far exceeded the original estimate (£175,000). It was opened on 1st July 1879, with stations at Aldridge, Streetly, Sutton Park, Sutton Coldfield and Penns, a distance of 12 miles 17.25 chains from Ryecroft to the triangular junction at Park Lane. It would, according to the "Walsall Observer", give people *"an opportunity of reaching the pretty and much frequented village of Aldridge, and the spacious parks and gardens of the royal town of Sutton"*. The Walsall-Sutton fare was 8d (3p) for 8 miles. Prior to 1879, the only rail journey from Walsall to Sutton, by the LNWR, was via Birmingham, a distance of 18.5 miles. On opening day the LNWR also reduced its fare to 8d.

There was some confusion at Walsall with the departure of the first train, as to who should announce it, the LNWR stationmaster or an official of the Midland Railway. After a some bluster from the stationmaster, the Midland official managed to do his duty. The arrival of the railway caused unemployment for at least one person -

"The Aldridge Coach Co. has proved very useful and convenient to many who have had no conveyance of their own to go to and from Aldridge. According to an advertisement in another column, now that the railway is open, the horses and omnibus of this company will be sold by auction on Monday week".

The same edition of the paper advertised Cook's Excursions by the new route to Alton Towers, Malvern and the Crystal Palace, with a daily 2pm excursion from Wolverhampton to Streetly and Sutton Park. One wildly optimistic feature of the time-table was the expectation that a separate Walsall - Water Orton service could be justified, for connection with services to Burton and Derby. On opening there were four such trains each way, but they had ceased by 1892.

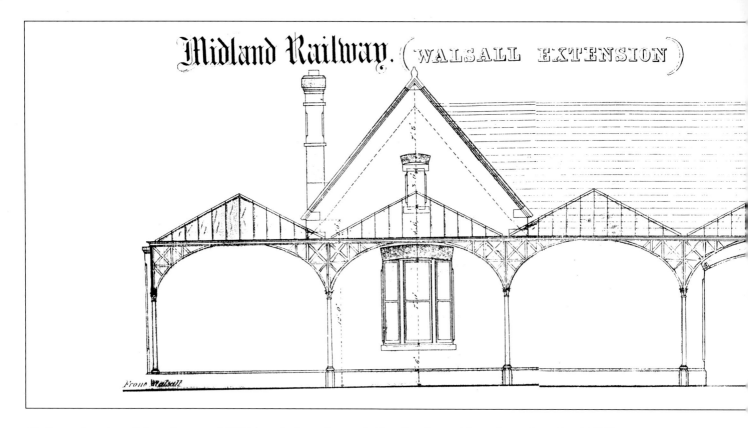

Platform elevation of the rather grand "Waiting sheds on the up platform" at Sutton Town, from plans dated 1877.

(Birmingham Library Services, Sutton Coldfield Library)

Aldridge, Streetly and Penns each had a standardised building on the up 'to Birmingham' platform. It had the appearance of two large cottages, end-on to the platform, one serving as a ladies' waiting room, the other as the booking office. They were joined together by a general waiting room with a ticket window. The down platform had a small brick shelter. Sutton Park had large buildings on its up island platform and on the down platform. Aldridge and Penns have been demolished, Sutton Park is decaying. Streetly is no longer recognisable, converted to a garage workshop and about to be demolished (1996). The exception in every sense is Sutton Coldfield. The main buildings and booking hall were entered from Midland Drive, on the 'to Walsall' platform. This station was more convenient for the town centre than Sutton Park. At the grouping the LMS renamed this station Sutton Coldfield Town to distinguish it from the LNWR station on the Lichfield line, although the Midland had sometimes referred to it as Sutton Town, as on plans for its construction, drawn up in 1877. The booking office may have been on the Walsall platform, but Birmingham passengers could not be denied their comforts. They had a building similar in appearance to that on the opposite platform. There were single sex waiting rooms at each end, plus toilets, joined by a general waiting room 44 feet 6 inches long. An added embellishment was the glass canopy which extended for the whole frontage of the building, 106 feet 3inches. The LMS soon decided that two town centre stations was one too many and that the Midland station would close. It was said that Sutton did not need two services to Birmingham, but this carefully ignored the fact that this line also provided direct trains to Walsall. No proper case was made for the closure and a 566 signature petition, presented by the Borough Council to the LMS in December 1924, was ignored.

The station closed on New Year's Day 1925. Although the first casualty, it is the last to survive in reasonable condition. The 'to Birmingham' building has been reduced to a shell but the main building, on Midland Drive, remains largely intact. Since closure it has seen a variety of uses - employment exchange, hairdressing salon - and now offices.

The line's passenger service, adequate but never lavish, was decimated during the Second World War and never improved afterwards. The potential at Aldridge, for example, with a rapidly expanding population and no direct bus link with Birmingham, was never exploited. It was no coincidence that a Birmingham bus service, provided weeks after the withdrawal of the trains, was an immediate success. Today the Sutton Park line remains as an important freight route, but those who are familiar with its history - or who remember what it was like to be a Scout or Guide - will know that its moment of glory came in the summer of 1957.

Their Finest Hour

During August 1957 Sutton Park was the scene of the "World Jubilee Jamboree of the Scout Movement" to celebrate its fiftieth anniversary. No other scouting occasion has ever matched it in size or scale. Planning began in 1955 and Sutton Park was chosen because it was a huge natural open space, with easy access and capable of accommodating large numbers of people who would be camping. The majority of Scouts and Guides would arrive by train, at Sutton Park, Streetly, or Sutton Coldfield. The Jamboree itself lasted from 1st to 12th August, but special trains began arriving on 29th July - at the rate of one every twelve minutes!

Just over a year earlier, in March 1956, a half-hourly service

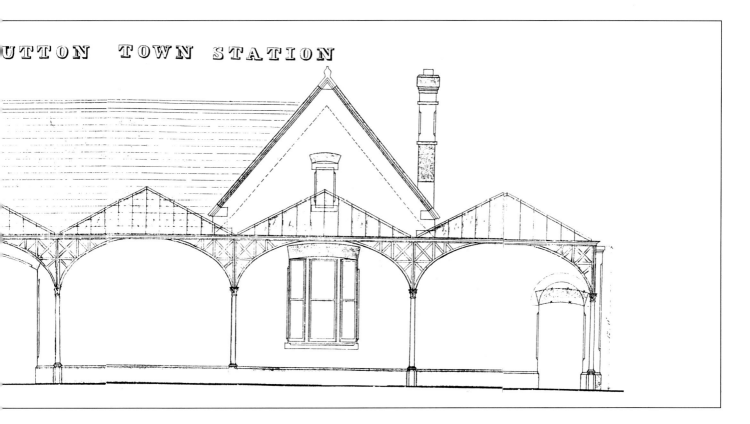

had begun between Sutton Coldfield and Birmingham, using the first diesel multiple units in the Midlands. Because of this frequent local service, it made sense to concentrate the Jamboree trains on the park line. Sutton Park and Streetly unknowingly received their last lick of paint and, more importantly, temporary signals and block posts were installed at Streetly and Penns. The block post signal cabin at Penns was an asbestos lined lamp storage hut. The outer face of the island platform at Streetly had long since been reclaimed by nature, but both sides of the island platform remained in use at Sutton Park, making it easier for some of the excursions and extra local trains to terminate there.

Over 130 special trains, from all parts of the country, brought Scouts to the Jamboree and took them all away again by August 14th. They were pulled by a wide variety of express steam types, especially Black 5s, Jubilees, Royal Scots and BR Standard Britannias. Three appropriate visitors were Royal Scots No.46168 "The Girl Guide", No.46169 "The Boy Scout" and Britannia No.70045 "Lord Rowallan", who was Chief Scout at the time, having named the loco at Euston on July 16th. "Lord Rowallan" left St.Pancras for Sutton Park at 10.35am on August 1st, with a special which signified the official opening of the Jamboree. Scouts and Guides had to rely on their parents for funding to get to the Jamboree - sponsorship was virtually unheard of - which is why many came from the USA, Canada and even Australia, but only a handful from poorer countries. It is believed that Thailand was represented by just two individuals. Within the camp there were many attractions, including an 'industrial pavilion' with a stand on locomotive building exhibiting models of steam, diesel and electric locomotives built in the UK and exported to all parts of the world. Locomotive building was still a substantial British industry and work on the railway was still seen as an attractive career with prospects.

Tuesday 6th August was Wolf Cub Day and 30,000 cubs arrived on site, 10,000 in coaches and the rest in 23 special trains. As well as the special trains to the Jamboree, there was a total of 97 day excursions from it. For instance, it was possible to go from Sutton Park to Bournville (for Cadburys), from Streetly to Crewe (for a tour of the locomotive works), from Sutton Coldfield to Coventry (to see the new cathedral under construction). Some trains went further afield, to London, Oxford or the North Wales resorts. As the "Railway Magazine" noted:- *"... a special railway office at the Jamboree was linked to the L.M.R. teleprinter network so that rapid arrangements could be made for the scouts' travel requirements through District offices in all parts of the Region".*

The Jamboree was open to the public every day between noon and 10pm. Admission was half a crown (12.5p) or one shilling (5p) for Scouts and Guides of any age in uniform. To cope with the daily visitors the Sutton Park local service was lavish indeed. All trains were steam hauled, normally with a minimum of four non-corridor carriages. Four 2-6-2 Class 2 tank engines and one Standard 2-6-0 Class 2 were loaned to Ryecroft specially to work this local service. (They were 41212, 41220, 41224, 41320 and 78055.) There was an hourly all-stations service between New Street and Walsall, with most trains extended to Wolverhampton via Pleck. An all-stations Sutton Park - Walsall - Dudley service ran every two hours. The first train along the line left Walsall at 06.25, the last at 22.05. August 13th and 14th saw two days of intense activity as Scouts and Guides were dispersed by special trains. As with the evening rush hour out from city centres, dispersal was more concentrated than arrival and long queues built up at all three stations. Everyone had previously been issued, airline style, with a boarding card, coloured according to their station of departure - blue for Sutton Park, yellow for Streetly and red for Sutton Coldfield. Such was the anticipated congestion that they were advised to 'check in' an hour before departure time, reduced to 40 minutes at Streetly.

As the final special left with the last scouts on the evening of August 14th peace returned to the Sutton Park line. It was however, the peace of neglect. The service was dieselised but otherwise unimproved. There was no surprise and little comment when it was withdrawn at the height of the Beeching era, in January 1965.

(Above)
A cheerfully busy scene on the down 'to Walsall' platform at Sutton Park during the Scouting Jamboree of August 1957.

(courtesy of Birmingham Library Services, Sutton Colfield Library)

(Opposite, lower)
An empty eastbound excursion train restarts from a signal check at Streetly, 7.03pm on Sunday 4th August 1957. Stanier Black 5 No.45333 hauls a short rake of just eight carriages in maroon livery. The station has received a fresh lick of paint, including both types of gas lamp, and new signs number the platforms. Two temporary signals and their cabin are in view. A small gaggle of scouts turns its back to the crossing and the special train departure board, which appeared to have its own gas lamp.

(Michael Mensing)

A double-headed excursion returning from the Jamboree to Stockport, with fifteen coaches on, pauses at Streetly at 7.35pm, Sunday 4th August 1957. Ivatt 2-6-0 Class 4, No.43022 pilots Stanier Black 5 No.45403. The ex-LMS carriages are still in 'blood and custard' livery, which was being superseded by all-over maroon by this time. The platform fencing is of Midland Railway pattern.

(Michael Mensing)

More Recent History

At the time of the Jamboree, there were further plans for the Sutton Park line. In steam days the well-maintained track had a line speed of 60mph. The main summit at Aldridge is approached by a continous gradient from Ryecroft, almost three miles, with over a mile at 1:100. Apart from a rising mile at 1:118 at Streetly, and a shallow rising gradient at Penns, the profile from Aldridge to Park Lane Junction falls continously, with two mile long stretches at 1:100. Because of the condition of the track and the gradient profile, the route was selected for high speed test running, and brake testing at speed, of the new diesel types then being developed. The up track (Walsall - Sutton - Park Lane Junction) was relaid with concrete sleepers and welded rail, which is still in use almost forty years later, and the line speed raised to 90mph. The down line was relaid with conventional bullhead rail and the line speed raised to 75mph. The new diesel types underwent trials on the line, including the Midland Blue Pullman, which began running between Snow Hill and Paddington in 1960. This overlapped with traditional steam activity, as recounted by G.Hopkinson, Saltley fireman and later guard during the 1960s. The itinerary of one pick-up goods trip working was as follows - light engine from Saltley to Bromford, shunt Dunlops sidings, trip to Water Orton, then along the Sutton Park line, compelled to fly shunt at Penns because of the cramped yard layout, shunt at Sutton Park and Aldridge, back light engine to Sutton Park to be relieved by the afternoon men, who had travelled 'on the cushions' from Vauxhall (a short walk from Saltley shed) to Sutton Coldfield (a similar walk from Sutton Park). Normal locos for this trip were ex-Midland 0-6-0s, numbered 44xxx by BR.

Once the testing of new diesels had been phased out, maintenance of the track declined. Over succeeding years the line speed was dropped in stages to 45mph, at which it remains. There was a 20mph restriction for no fewer than 4 miles through Sutton Park station and the state of the track was so bad that a train was derailed.

However, track is now being progressively relaid and it is planned to raise the line speed to 75mph by the year 2000. This will make it easier to reinstate a passenger service in the future. It would be of particular use to Aldridge, where the station site is ideally placed for the town centre, and where there is room for a large car park. Like Aldridge, Penns has also been the scene of much housing development since the station closed. Beyond Park Lane Junction local station(s) could be strategically placed on the Midland line into New Street to serve Castle Vale, a huge development of the 1960s in dire need of a quick and efficient public transport link with Birmingham city centre.

Walsall Power Box controls the Sutton Park line as far as Streetly, where Saltley Power Box takes charge. Extra signals have been inserted on the westbound line to shorten the sections and so keep traffic moving freely on what is still a busy freight line, which sees more trains during the night than in the daytime. Typical traffics include steel trains from Tees-side to Wolverhampton, oil trains from Ellesmere Port and the Freightliner service between Birmingham Lawley Street and Glasgow via Crewe.

During the Second World War, Sutton Park station became a mail centre. It was originally a US Army sorting office for the large numbers of US servicemen billetted in the park itself. After the war it was converted for use as a Royal Mail Divisional Sorting Office, based at the mail buildings and sidings on the south side of the station. The overnight mail trains running to or through New Street would each detach at least one van for Sutton Park. Local mail, from passenger trains, would also be transferred and a morning mail train, normally consisting of six vans, would be formed at New Street and leave for Sutton Park. The train loco remained there until 10am to sort and shunt the vans as necessary, with the Post Office paying BR for use of the loco and its crew. From Sutton Park the mail was distributed by road. Each evening the pattern operated in reverse, with the train leaving for New Street at 18.15.

42429 arrives at Sutton Park with a mixed bag of carriages on 25th July 1955. The train was the 5.17pm from Wolverhampton to New Street via Willenhall and Walsall.

(Roger Carpenter)

Sutton Park was also important as an international sorting depot, with surface mail arriving on regular trains from, amongst other places, Southampton Docks. I was told by G.Hopkinson, working as a guard, about the Whitemoor-Curzon Street fitted freight, which he joined at Leicester. This train had vehicles carrying mail from Felixstowe docks. Normally it passed through Sutton Park without stopping, detaching the mail vans at Bescot for them to be tripped back later the same day. There seemed, to him, to be no logic in this arrangement, so he always arranged for the train to stop and the vans to be detached. Charlie, the Sutton Park shunter, once told him that the mails were delivered a day earlier in consequence.

Rail borne mail journeys withered and finally ceased in 1991. The depot is now served entirely by road as the sidings gather rust. Remaining rail traffic is ferried to and from the large Royal Mail depot at Curzon Street, behind the surviving building of the London & Birmingham station.

CHAPTER FIVE : THE LNWR AT WALSALL
(A glimpse at some interesting features)

(South Staffordshire Legacy : Sister Dora : Further Expansion :
Thomas Hinckley, Railway Photographer : Walsall's New Station)

Much has already been written about the London & North Western Railway in earlier chapters and pictures of its locomotives, stations, etc. also occur elsewhere this book. To anyone reading "Rails Around Walsall" chronologically, it will be obvious by now that the LNWR was the dominant railway in the area, no more so than in Walsall itself ....

South Staffordshire Legacy
The LNWR absorbed the South Staffordshire Railway in July 1867, although the lease was transferred from John Robinson McClean in 1861, effectively killing the South Staffs' independent existence. In 1855 the South Staffs had obtained an Act for two Black Country loop lines - it was left to the LNWR to construct and operate them.

The Darlaston Loop was two and a half miles long, leaving the Grand Junction line at James Bridge and joining the South Staffs at Wednesbury. It opened in September 1863. Motorway junctions today are a magnet for industrial estates and warehousing; this line was a nineteenth century equivalent. The loop stimulated further growth in what was already an industrial area, with private sidings serving Lloyds Steelworks, timber yards and, of course, Wednesbury Patent Shaft works. The single track loop had to be doubled in 1872. The line has now entirely gone, a victim of the decline of both railfreight and heavy industry. The complete loop remained open until 1963 and the last section, to the Patent Shaft, lingered as a private siding until 1980.

Passenger trains ran between Wednesbury, on the South Staffs, and James Bridge, on the Grand Junction. The only station actually on the loop was Darlaston itself. The passenger service opened with no fewer than 56 trains each way daily, which had declined to 15 by 1877. It was withdrawn in November 1887 and Darlaston station platforms were demolished in 1889. Darlaston had the dubious distinction of being about the first station in the country to close because of apparent tramway competition. Not nice clean new-fangled electric trams either, like the ones first seen at Blackpool in 1883, but the slow and smoky steam trams that began a Wednesbury - Darlaston - Walsall service in 1884. It was rare for them to exceed 12mph. The closure of a station in the 1880s was a highly unusual event, with no proper procedure for public objections etc. Eventually a dispute, between the Darlaston Local Board and the LNWR, reached the Royal Courts of Justice, where a judgment was given on 21st December 1893.

(A copy of the complete document is kept in Walsall Local History Centre.) The Board sought to compel the LNWR to restore the service but this was refused. A legal precedent was thus created, that the courts had no power to force a railway to restore a closed passenger service. In his judgment Mr.Justice Wills was influenced by the fact that Wednesbury and James Bridge stations were both less than a mile from the Bull Stake, the recognised centre of Darlaston. Reading the full text it appears that tramway competition was as much of a pretext as a genuine reason for closure, so that the heavy mineral traffic could flow unimpeded. The LNWR was criticised for failing to produce proper statistics to reinforce its case. The company placed undue track charges on the local trains - *"I look myself with .... some suspicion upon the division of expenses which allocates the maintenance of the permanent way to the light passenger traffic"* - in a way which became depressingly familiar in more recent times. The local board was also reminded of its place in the scheme of things - *"I wish to give no countenance to the notion that a place like Darlaston, with a comparatively small population, and with very moderate needs in respect of traffic, making a very moderate contribution to the exchequer of the Railway Company, can for a moment expect to be treated as if they were the most important part of the service of the Company."* And there the matter ended. The people of Darlaston could continue to use Wednesbury station until July 1964 and James Bridge (renamed Darlaston in 1913) until January 1965. Parts of the trackbed remain near the town centre and Darlaston still has its Station Street.

The Princes End branch opened on the same day as the Darlaston Loop. There were two intermediate stations, Princes End (1863) and Ocker Hill (1864). LNWR line local trains between Walsall and Wolverhampton were all routed this way until the opening of the curves at Pleck and Portobello in 1881. After that, daily trains along the branch were reduced to three in each direction and they were withdrawn in 1890. The local authority at Tipton fought hard for the trains to be restored and - unlike Darlaston - it was successful. The service reopened in 1895 but there were never more than five trains in each direction and it closed as a wartime economy, on 1st January 1916. As with the Darlaston Loop, the Princes End line, which was always double track, was important for freight. Its triangular junction with the Stour Valley at Tipton gave it greater flexibility. Trains

An unidentified Class 45 'Peak' eases its train of empty bogie tanks off the spur to Wednesbury Steel Terminal, summer 1977. Ocker Hill Power Station forms the backdrop.

(John Whitehouse)

between Stewart & Lloyds Steelworks at Bilston and the South Staffs line were routed via Princes End. Electrification works in the 1960s meant that InterCity trains were sometimes diverted over the line. The mothballing of Ocker Hill coal-fired power station, followed by the demise of Stewart & Lloyds in 1979, spelt the end, and the line was closed in 1980.

Sister Dora

Dorothy Wyndlow Pattison was the daughter of the Rector of Hauxwell, a village in the North Riding of Yorkshire. She first came to Walsall, for just two months, early in 1865. By this time she was 33 years old and a member of Christ Church Sisterhood, an order of nursing sisters within the Church of England. As such she took the name of Sister Dora, which she kept even after she left the sisterhood in 1875. At the end of 1865 she returned to Walsall and settled there permanently. Her energy, devotion to duty and ability to influence or cajole those best able to help her, meant that her campaign for a proper hospital for the town was successful when facilities were expanded from the cramped Cottage Hospital to include The Mount, a former private school, in 1868. She was given overall responsibility for the running of the hospital and it seemed to some of the patients - whose written testimonies survive - that she was always around, whatever the hour, to attend to their needs. Among many acts of great courage, she comforted relatives of the 22 men entombed when

Pelsall Hall Colliery flooded in 1872 and for almost five months in 1875 she alone tended the sick and dying at the Isolation Hospital during an outbreak of smallpox. Not surprisingly she was compared with Florence Nightingale.

Her work brought her into contact with those suffering from industrial injuries, including railwaymen. Industrial accidents were common, generating the majority of patients in any given year. There were 177 patients admitted during 1871, 17 died and of these 5 were "railway servants injured on the line". The Annual Report for 1874 stated-

"For several months there was a strike in the coal trade, whereby not only a large number of miners, but also iron-workers, were thrown out of employment, and the traffic on the railway considerably reduced; and as the railway, iron works and mines are the three great sources whence most of the accidents come, the suspension of work in connection with these great undertakings reduced the number of patients from accidents. The number of in-patients in the past year was 197, against 239 in the previous year."

On one occasion a ticket collector was killed in an accident at Walsall station. His children called at the hospital, in great distress, hoping to see their father's body, but Sister Dora forbade it, knowing that its mutilated condition would only add to their agony. At midnight, her many other duties finished, she went to the mortuary and *"made his features presentable, so that the*

Sister Dora poses for the camera outside Walsall Cottage Hospital, 20th June 1873. She has just been presented with a pony and trap by local LNWR railwaymen.

(Walsall Local History Centre)

spectacle was not so shocking", making sure that the children came to see their father the following day. The hospital, like all hospitals of the time, continued to rely completely for its income on gifts and subscriptions. Of the £340 donated during 1876, £4 was raised through a collecting box at Walsall station.

To show their appreciation of her work, some LNWR railwaymen contributed from their wages to raise a sum of £50, which was spent on presenting her, in June 1873, with a pony and trap, which she used on her rounds visiting the sick. She lived just long enough to see the opening of the large new Cottage Hospital in November 1878, dying of breast cancer a few weeks later, on Christmas Eve, aged 46. The whole town came to a standstill for her funeral, at which the coffin was carried by eighteen railwaymen, in uniform, from the house on the Wednesbury Road where she had died. A statue of Sister Dora has stood in the centre of Walsall, in the square known as The Bridge, since 1886.

In 1895 a member of the 2-4-0 "Jumbo" Class, No.2158, was named "Sister Dora". Thomas Hinckley's photograph shows it at Bescot, ready to depart for Birmingham. It was based at the small LNWR shed at Derby. Between 1896 and 1906 its normal diagram, six days per week, was to work the morning Derby to Walsall train, which ran via Burton, Birmingham New Street and the Soho Loop. After arrival, it travelled light engine to Ryecroft shed, where any necessary cleaning or routine maintenance was carried out. In the evening, "Sister Dora" worked the return train to Derby. Throughout this period the

loco had one regular driver, Charles Sayer. Jack Haddock, living near Ryecroft, recalled staff from the 1930s who knew both loco and driver. Sayer seemed to regard the engine almost as his personal property. He could be seen polishing the nameplate at each visit to Ryecroft. He never used the messroom but always ate lunch - his 'snap' - on the footplate as though he were guarding the engine. Whenever the shed fitter made running repairs or minor adjustments, Sayer watched him closely, polishing away his fingerprints afterwards.

In 1977 Jack Haddock met two railway inspectors, based at Walsall and New Street, to discuss his idea of reviving the Sister Dora name in time to commemorate the centenary of her death. The Chairman of British Rail was aware of this and seemed happy to agree, but nothing was done, despite the support of the local MP. In 1988 a committee was formed to organise the first Open Day at Bescot and they successfully applied for permission for a loco to be named. The naming took place at the Open Day, Sunday 9th October 1988, and the loco concerned was one of the so-called "Bescot Castles", No.31 430. The ceremony was performed by Mrs.Ros Parkes, Vice-Chair of Walsall Health Authority. Subsequent Bescot Open Days saw the naming of other Class 31s after Walsall people; in 1990 No.31 423 became "Jerome K.Jerome", the Victorian author of 'Three Men in a Boat'; in 1992 No.31 107 received the name "John H.Carless VC", after a naval gunner, born in Walsall in 1896, who continued to fight bravely, despite fatal injuries, in a battle off Heligoland in 1917.

"Jumbo" Class No.2158 was named "Sister Dora" when it was built in 1895. It is seen here, in its usual beautiful condition, around 1903, about to leave Bescot with a local train for New Street.   *(Thomas Hinckley; Roger Carpenter collection)*

Prior to the first Open Day efforts had been made to trace any descendants of Charles Sayer, without success. Four years later Jack Haddock was working at Walsall Local History Centre when, by a remarkable coincidence, he was introduced to Leslie Sayer, who proved to be Charles' great-great grandson. In October 1995, at Transrail's invitation, Leslie Sayer was invited to Bescot to inspect the locomotive, so maintaining his family's links with both Walsall and "Sister Dora". Although the loco was subsequently withdrawn the name was transferred to another Bescot engine, 37 116 which, in the best tradition of its predecessors, is kept in immaculate condition. (See back cover).

Further Expansion

In October 1877 a new LNWR engine shed was opened at Walsall, replacing the earlier South Staffs shed, which had opened in 1840 and was situated a little to the south, nearer the station. The new shed was officially 'Walsall', but always known as Ryecroft, being situated between the Cannock and Lichfield lines at that unique four-way junction. It was a standard shed of the period, with twelve roads designed to stable 48 passenger and freight locomotives. Except for the addition of a turntable and coaling tower, it remained largely unaltered throughout its existence. It was such an important institution in the railway life of Walsall until well within living memory that part of Chapter Six is devoted to the photographs and memories of some of those who worked there. Ryecroft is mentioned here merely to establish its beginnings.

The same is true for Bescot. In Grand Junction days it was the site of Walsall's first station, and the scene of some freight activity thanks to Edward Elwell's Wednesbury Forge. It became a junction with the opening of the South Staffs line, but its strategic importance was not fully established until the opening of the first marshalling yard here in December 1881, on a site now occupied by part of the up yard. The industries of the Black Country and the output of the South Staffordshire coalfield were expanding rapidly and extra sorting sidings were added throughout the 1880s. Trains arrived and departed in increasing numbers, and the expanding yard needed a stud of shunting locomotives and somewhere to house them. This busy site was a focus for considerable activity, but all the motive power was based elsewhere, leading to much wasteful light engine running between the yard, Ryecroft and other neighbouring sheds. The situation was remedied with the opening of an eight road engine shed in 1892. (Further sorting sidings, on the down side of the main line, were opened in October of that year.) Freight and shunting locomotives could now be based here and those bringing trains in for sorting could be serviced and refuelled.

Bescot shed and yard are part of railway legend. The yard is still one of the most important in the country and the shed has been succeeded by Bescot Traction Maintenance Depot (TMD). The development of Bescot during the twentieth century is featured in Chapter Six.

Another important addition to the LNWR network at this time was the Soho Loop line. It is impossible to improve on Rex Christiansen's definition in "A Regional History of the Railways of Great Britain" (Volume 7) - *"Few, if any, lines developed after the main system were to be as valuable as the short link between Soho and Perry Barr"*.

The loop forms a link between the Stour Valley and Grand Junction lines and has the virtue of double-facing junctions at both ends. It opened to goods traffic in 1888 and to passengers on 1st April 1889. That date also saw the opening of a newly quadrupled section of the Stour Valley between the junction with the Harborne branch and the new loop line. The Soho Loop had an important goods branch to Soho Pool, containing thirteen long sidings with a capacity of almost 500 wagons. It closed in 1974, except for a remnant which served the Texaco oil terminal until 1984. On opening to passengers the only intermediate station

One of the Class 31 'Bescot Castles', 31 430, was named "Sister Dora" at a ceremony during the Bescot Open Day of 9th October 1988.
(Stephen Widdowson)

was at Soho Road. It was joined by Handsworth Wood in 1896. Both stations closed as a wartime economy in 1941. Throughout their existence trains were infrequent and many of them provided a circle service, New Street to New Street via the loop and Aston. The loop is electrified and is now used by some of the Walsall line trains.

The real importance of the Soho Loop was - and is - as a strategic freight route, relieving pressures on other lines and enabling freight trains to avoid New Street station. It is one of several such lines that remain in the Birmingham area. Other examples include the Aston - Stechford line and the short link between Landor Street and St.Andrew's junctions.

Thomas Hinckley, Railway Photographer

A characteristic of many railwaymen is their enthusiasm for their work. To many it would seem to be a paid hobby! One such was Thomas Hinckley, a platelayer with the LNWR who was based at Walsall for several years near the beginning of the twentieth century. He combined the love of his work with a keen interest in photography, taking pictures with his quarter plate camera in the Walsall area between 1902 and 1905. His work gave him access to parts of the railway denied to others. In view of the strict discipline relating to working practices at the time, his superiors must have turned an indulgent blind eye when they saw him lugging his equipment across the tracks - perhaps they admired the results of his previous efforts, especially if they had posed for his camera? He captured the everyday railway at work, both trains and people. He managed successful pictures of locos at speed, a great skill with the camera technology of the time. As a platelayer his hobby would probably have been seen by some of his workmates as eccentric - class prejudices quickly bubbling to the surface - and the expense of buying the equipment, improvising a dark room, etc., would have strained his modest pay packet. I am indebted to Roger Carpenter for allowing me to use these pictures which first appeared, with others, in his "L&NWR West Midlands Album". Roger makes the point that we cannot be totally sure that the pictures are by Hinckley, although there is very small room for doubt.

At this time many professional artists and photographers were arguing passionately whether photography could be considered as a true art form. Charles Holme wrote in the Summer 1905 edition of "Studio" magazine -

"It is now possible to tell a photograph by almost any leading and well-known worker at a glance, to distinguish the style easily ...... This fact not only lends dignity to the works themselves, but also forms the strongest possible argument that Photography, like all arts, is evolutionary, and in a word - is an art".

It is unlikely that Thomas Hinckley was a subscriber to "Studio", but the point is well made - he was an artist.

Locomotive No.2060 "Vandal" (a name that would definitely not be chosen today), stands at the north end of Platform 3, Walsall, some time before July 1904, when it was scrapped. This was one of Francis Webb's three cylinder compound engines of the "Dreadnought" class. These 40 express locomotives were built in 1884-88 and relegated to local passenger duties towards the end of their lives. As the driving wheels were not coupled, their grip on the road, when starting with a heavy train, was not as sure as it might have been. The train crew has been 'visited' by colleagues for photographic purposes, while an unseen hand seems to be cleaning out the guards van. The bulge at the train end of this vehicle contains slim side windows, enabling the guard to view the whole train without putting his head out of the window. The covered way linking the booking hall with the platforms frames the top of this picture. A short rake of parcels vans rests in the Cannock bay.

(*Thomas Hinckley; Roger Carpenter collection*)

50

Locomotive No.860 "Merrie Carlisle", of the Renewed Precedent Class, a 2-4-0 express passenger type famous for smart running on the West Coast Main Line, seen here on lighter duties at Walsall, about 1903. The white disc on the cab roof displays '14', the number for Stafford shed. The booking hall on the right was built when the station was enlarged in 1884. It was destroyed by fire in 1916 and replaced by the famous 'drum' in 1923. Beneath it lurks the station signal box. Because of its appallingly polluted location inside Park Street Tunnel, no signalman was allowed to operate the box for more than nine months. One item of non-standard equipment fixed to a wall bracket was a small dinghy, a means of escape from the sudden and deep floods to which the station was prone.

(Thomas Hinckley; Roger Carpenter collection)

A southbound Grand Junction express rattles over the points at Bescot, hauled by a   2-4-0 "Jumbo" No.868 "Condor", about 1903. To the left is Bescot Junction No.3 signal box, replaced by another mechanical box as late as 1952. The photographer was positioned at the north end of Bescot's down platform and the train was a Wolverhampton - Euston express.

(Thomas Hinckley; Roger Carpenter collection)

A southbound train at Bescot, about 1903. The express headcode of one lamp above each buffer means that it may well be a businessman's train between Walsall and New Street, calling only at Bescot and Aston. The locomotive is one of a goods class introduced in 1880 by Francis Webb. They soon proved adept at passenger work as well. They were the first engines to use David Joy's valve gear, patented in 1879, which improved the distribution of steam to the cylinders and hence the 'balance' of the loco when running. They were also the first to use the company crest which - from a distance - resembled a cauliflower and gave rise to their nickname. This "Cauliflower" is No.672.

(Thomas Hinckley; Roger Carpenter collection)

Walsall's New Station

Walsall's South Staffs station, dating from 1849, had just two platforms with two running lines. In 1861 space between the platforms was increased and goods lines laid through the station area. By 1879 the network of lines into Walsall was complete, but the station still had just two platforms! It was rebuilt and enlarged and the work completed in November 1883. The main entrance and booking hall was now on Park Street and there were five platforms and two north facing bays. The platform buildings were of the LNWR standard type, of the sort that can still be seen at a few stations in the area, notably Sutton Coldfield and Lichfield City. By the beginning of the twentieth century the station was handling about a thousand train movements per day and was the focus of employment for over two hundred people. The booking hall was damaged by fire in March 1916. The roof, beyond repair, had to be patched up until the end of the war, when it was decided to replace the whole hall and carry out other improvements.

So, the last act of the LNWR, insofar as Walsall was concerned, was the planning of this new entrance and booking hall. The drawings reproduced on pages 54-55 and inside the cover of this book were dated 17th August 1922. The Railways Act of 19th August 1921 provided for the grouping of virtually all railway companies into the 'Big Four'. The LNWR and Midland were to form part of the London Midland & Scottish Railway. The Act was effective from New Year's Day 1923, so the improvements were completed by the LMS. And what improvements they were!

The Park Street entrance was reached through a glass canopied portico, 70 feet wide and 26 feet deep, with a height of 26 feet to the apex of the roof. The booking hall was semi-circular at the rear, with an off-centre entrance to the widened covered way, which led to the footbridge serving all platforms. The hall floor area consisted of a rectangle, 70 feet by 35 feet, with a semi-circle at the rear, 35 in radius. The entrance doors, 11 feet tall, were of solid oak, panelled, with roundels for decoration. Similar panels lined all the walls and there was a beautiful panelled ceiling, 19 feet above the floor. Greek-style pillars supported the roof, which contained three large leaded windows. An amenity appreciated by one railwayman, but unnoticed by virtually everyone using the station, was a ventilation duct for the station signal box, let into the booking hall floor.

The hall was officially opened at 8am on Sunday 4th November 1923. The entrance doors were pushed aside by J.F.Bradford, District Superintendent at Birmingham, and a celebration breakfast was enjoyed in the station restaurant by the official party. Mr.Bradford said, "The LMS desires to do all it can to assist in promoting the welfare of the town" and appealed to people not to damage the stonework by striking matches on it. W.A.Thomas, the Goods Manager at Wolverhampton, added that there were few stations which had such a fine approach and the hall would unquesionably be the envy of neighbouring towns - Wolverhampton was already pressing for improvements of its own. The improvements at Walsall had cost £25,000 and had used local labour. The building contract was awarded to a Coventry firm, and the steel was milled in Darlaston.

This fine building served the station well for over fifty years. It was one of Walsall's landmarks. In 1978, against all the rules of common sense and good taste, it was demolished, along with the original South Staffs building in Station Street. It made way for a nondescript shopping centre, whose brutal concrete rear was the first thing to assault the eyes of people arriving by train from Birmingham. Platform buildings were swept away, to be replaced by tacky little cabins. Walsall station has never fully recovered from this vandalism, although recent improvements have been thoughtful and well-meaning and the approach from within the shopping centre is pleasant. However, instead of being obvious from Park Street, the latest station buildings still cower below the shopping centre; a stranger to the town would scarcely know that a station was there.

Walsall station, looking north along Platform 2, about 1910. The light engine, a 'Cauliflower', masks the view of a train with Midland Railway carriages standing at Platform 1.

(Bill Mayo collection)

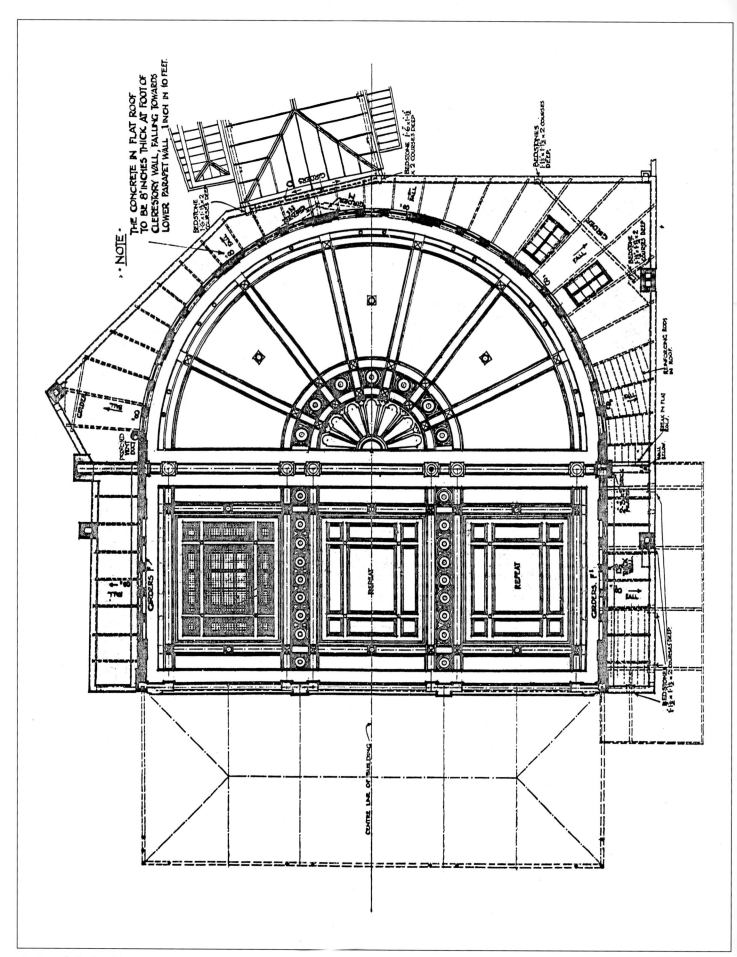

A plan of the booking hall ceiling at Walsall station, 1922.

(courtesy of Railtrack)

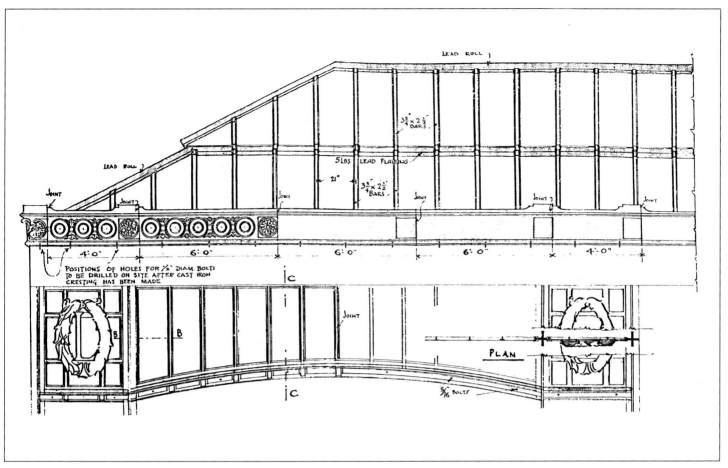

Plans for improvements to Walsall station, showing details of the Park Street entrance canopy. *(courtesy of Railtrack)*

One photograph which captures some of the many faces of Walsall station under water, 28th January 1978. The South Staffordshire Railway buildings can be seen midway along Platform 1, flanked by later LNWR additions. The semi-circular shape of the 1923 booking hall is visible beyond the steps. The buildings on the island platform, although beneath criticism, were the only ones not demolished later that year. *(D.Beech)*

A Fowler tank loco draws into Platform 1, Walsall, with an excursion train, around 1934. The destination is unknown but the weather is set fair, everyone looks happy, and with the platform clock showing 11.25 they would not have too far to go.

(Walsall Local History Centre)

It would be difficult to look at this picture and argue that the rebuilding of Walsall station in 1978 was an improvement. The earlier London & North Western platform buildings had been neglected for years, but an opportunity was missed when they were replaced by the appalling structures seen here. The multi-storey car park, on former railway land, had no access to the station, neither did the bus station behind it in Bradford Place. Access between bus/car park and train involved a walk through the town centre and the chance to link all three for the benefit of the travelling public was lost. A southbound tank train in charge of Bo-Bo diesel 25 289 passes alongside the redundant Platform 4, whilst a four car Class 310 emu waits with the 17.23 all stations to New Street, 14th September 1978. At the time Walsall 'enjoyed' an hourly service to Birmingham, with two extras each way in the morning and evening peaks.

(Michael Mensing)

This shot of the booking hall at Walsall station gives an idea of what was lost when the bulldozers moved in. Passengers progressed from the pair of ticket windows, let into the oak panelling, past the ticket inspector's booth to the covered way leading to the platforms. The double-sided notice board was a cheap lightweight replacement of an oak original. *(David Fink)*

Sulzer Bo-Bo diesel-electric 5292 approaches Walsall, south of Ryecroft, with a short fitted freight off the Sutton Park line on 16th May 1973. This section has since reverted to double track. Walsall Town Hall peeps above the white factory unit. *(Michael Mensing)*

Bescot as it was known and loved by generations of small boys before the end of steam. The locos are in the disposal area, in front of the unique Wellman Smith Owen mechanical coaling plant. Unusually, there is not a Super D in sight. Behind the station, Walsall Gas Works and Birchills Power Station stretch to the horizon. Photographed during the long hot summer of 1959. *(Jack Haddock)*

56 091 "Castle Donington Power Station", passes Bescot Stadium station with a northbound train for the Walsall line, Saturday 4th May 1996. Ballast wagons and stored tanks occupy the nearer part of the old down yard (left). The up yard contains a healthy quantity and variety of stock. The ribbon of colour leading to the horizon behind the down yard is the M6, which was at a standstill at the time.

(Author)

General Motors built Class 59, No.59 005, owned by Foster Yeomans and designed to haul long aggregate trains from their stone terminal at Merehead, Somerset, is on display at Bescot Open Day, 6th May 1990. With fine static exhibits like this, it is not surprising that each of Bescot's three open days (1988,1990,1992) raised many thousands of pounds in entrance money, all of which was donated to charity. *(Stephen Widdowson)*

31 102 "Cricklewood" stands within the Traction Maintenance Depot at Bescot, over the inspection pit on Road 4 and between the jacks which have a combined lift capacity of 100 tonnes, 24th May 1996. *(Author)*

The Grand Junction's viaduct over Lawley Street is still in good heart, despite its age and the imposition of an upper deck, added in 1893 on the approach to a new viaduct, built to carry the tracks into New Street above the congested throat of Curzon Street goods station. The 323 checked at the signal is a Birmingham Cross City train from Lichfield to Redditch, 24th May 1996. *(Author)*

323 208, on a Walsall-New Street service, crosses the bridge at Nechells Green as it slows for the stop at Duddeston, 24th May 1996.

(Author)

A two-car Birmingham RCW dmu pauses at Aldridge with the 2.45pm Sutton Park to Walsall train on Sunday 30th August 1964, less than six months before closure.
(Michael Mensing)

The Sutton Park line remains busy with freight. Over two miles of straight track run through the park itself, on a rising gradient of 1:165 towards Streetly. A Class 37 with a short train of empties approaches the site of Streetly station, 4th July 1996.
(Author)

A Class 310 emu passes the site of Handsworth Wood station, on the Soho Loop, with the 13.47 fast service from Walsall to New Street, 7th May 1996. *(Author)*

A Class 56, in Load Haul livery, leans to the curve through Handsworth Park, on the Soho Loop, with its train of empty continous-welded-rail bogies, 7th May 1996. *(Author)*

Two pictures which show something of the basic nature of the stations along the Cannock line. Between re-opening in 1989 and the extension of the service to Rugeley, all trains arrived at, and departed from, the former up platform at Hednesford. The 11.53 to New Street is seen leaving (above) on 9th July 1996. A little over two hours later, the 13.53 to New Street leaves Bloxwich, a little to the north of the original station. *(Author)*

Fosseway Crossing, near Hammerwich, on 5th March 1970. BR Class 128 parcels car M55994 braves the wind chill as it sprints towards Lichfield. It was one of six Inter-City parcels cars built by the Gloucester RCW Co. for the Western Region in 1959. Three pairs of sliding doors on each side eased rapid loading and unloading. The corridors meant that they could work in multiple with other members of the same class, enabling parcels to be sorted on the move. The corridors were not used after four units were transferred to the London Midland Region in the early 1960s. *(Michael Mensing)*

Charrington's Fuel Depot, Anglesey Sidings, shortly after the arrival of the overnight train from Immingham, 4th May 1996. The discharge pipes are heated, hence the steam, which envelops 60 070 "John Lauden McAdam" at the head of the right hand rake of tanks. The long shunting neck to the right marks the course of the line to Ryecroft. *(Author)*

CAUGHT IN TIME

Time-tables, schedules and excursions

(All time-table extracts and handbills reproduced in this feature are by courtesy of Robert Pearson)

BIRMINGHAM, SUTTON-COLDFIELD, WALSALL, and WOLVERHAMPTON.—Midland.

(Timetable extract — "Bradshaw", April 1910. Columns for Week Days and Sundays. Stations include Wellington Station, Leeds, Derby, London (St. Pancras), Leicester (Lon. Rd.), Birmingham (New St.), Saltley, Castle Bromwich, Penns, Sutton Coldfield, Sutton Park, Streetly, Aldridge, Walsall, North Walsall, Short Heath (Clark's Lane), Willenhall (Midland), Willenhall (L. & N. W.), Wednesfield, Wolverhampton. A second table shows the reverse direction from Wolverhampton High Level Station.)

Notes:
- a — Arrives 11 15 aft. on Saturdays.
- b — Arrives at 2 30 aft. on Saturdays.
- c — Mondays only.
- h — Arrives at 11 55 aft. on Thursdays and Saturdays.
- n — Except Mondays.
- o — Via Derby.
- L. & N. W. Trains.
- † — High Level.
- ‖ — About ½ mile to Snow Hill Station (G.W.).

☞ For other Trains
BETWEEN	PAGE
Birmingham and Castle Bromwich	572 to 583
Walsall and Wolverhampton	454 & 455

The Midland Railway's 25-mile route between Birmingham, Walsall and Wolverhampton is shown above ("Bradshaw", April 1910). The Walsall-Wolverhampton section saw Midland trains running over the LNWR route (eg. the 9.05am from Birmingham) and vice versa. The Walsall-Birmingham section was served exclusively by Midland trains, but showing Birmingham-London connections to St. Pancras via Leicester, whilst omitting reference to the LNWR service to Euston, seems to be stretching company loyalties, not to mention the gullibility of the travelling public!

A local train to Walsall on the Sutton Park line passes through the 'Blue Hole' cutting, between Aldridge and Ryecroft, one day during 1934.

(Frank Ash)

STAFFORD, RUGELEY, CANNOCK, and WALSALL.—London and North Western.

Miles	Up.	Week Days. mrn	mrn	mrn	mrn	mrn	mrn	mrn	non	aft	aft (Saturdays only.)	m (Except Saturdays.)	aft	aft	aft	aft	aft	Sundays. mrn	aft	aft	aft	aft
	Stafford ....dep.	6 45	....	....	8 2	9 0	1010	....	12 0	2 2	....	....	4 0	4 55	....	6 15	8 55	8 20	1225	....	....	7 45
4	Milford and Brocton	6 53	....	7 44	....	9 9	1019	....	12 9	2 10	....	....	4 8	5 3	....	6 24	9 3	8 30	....	....	....	7 54
6¼	Colwich	7 0	....	7 51	8 14	9 15	1025	....	12 15	2 16	3 20	3 20	4 14	5 8	....	7 5	9 8	8 38	....	3 25	....	8 4
9½	Rugeley (Trent Valley) arr.	7 5	....	7 59	8 18	9 22	1031	m	12 22	2 24	3 25	3 25	4 22	5 15	....	7 10	9 13	8 43	1243	3 30	m	8 9
	Rugeley (Trent Valley) dep.	7 7	....		8 26	9 34		11 20	12 27	2 40	3 35	3 35	4 35	5 30	m	7 28	9 22	8 46	....		3 50	8 12
10½	Rugeley Town....	7 10	....	Runs 15 minutes later on Mondays.	8 33	9 43	....	11 25	12 30	2 43	3 41	3 41	4 38	5 33	6 30	7 31	9 26	8 51	....	....	3 55	8 17
14¼	Hednesford	7 22	8 15		8 43	9 53	....	11 38	12 43	2 54	3 54	3 54	4 50	5 45	6 43	7 43	9 39	9 5	....	....	4 9	8 32
16¼	Cannock	7 27	8 20		8 48	9 58	....	11 43	12 48	2 59	3 59	3 59	4 55	5 50	6 48	7 48	9 44	9 10	....	....	4 14	8 38
18	Wyrley and Church Bridge ¶ .	7 31	8 24		8 52	10 2	....	11 47	12 52	3 3	4 3	4 3	4 59	5 54	6 52	7 52	9 48	9 15	....	....	4 18	8 43
21¼	Bloxwich	7 40	8 33		9 0	1012	....	11 57	1 0	3 11	4 14	4 14	5 7	6 4	7 4	8 0	9 56	9 26	....	....	4 30	8 57
22½	Birchills	....	....		....	....	....	12 0	....	....	....	4 17	....	....	7 7	....	....	....	....	....	4 33	....
24½	Walsall 447, 454, 455 ..arr.	7 48	8 41		9 8	1018	....	12 5	1 10	3 20	4 21	4 21	5 17	6 10	7 12	8 9	10 3	9 35	....	....	4 39	9 5
32½	454 Wolverhampton (H. L.) arr	8 43	....		9 31	1047	....	12‡37	2u24	3 48	4 50	4 50	6 4	6 47	8 16	8‡41	1031	1026	‡	....	7g49	1019g
35½	455 Birmingham (New St.). "	8 29	....		9 50	1050	....	12v35	2 0	4 6	4 50	4 50	6 11	6 50	7 56	9 5	11 5	1025	....	....	5 28	9 58

g Via Dudley Port.
m Motor Car, one class only.
u Arrives at 1 49 aft. on Saturdays; 1st and 3rd class.
v Arrives at 12 55 aft. on Saturdays.
‡ 1st and 3rd class.
¶ "Halt" at Landywood, between Wyrley and Church Bridge and Bloxwich.

For other Trains

BETWEEN PAGE
Stafford and Rugeley (Trent Valley) .... 413 to 419

L. & N. W.

The April 1910 "Bradshaw" shows a through service between Walsall, Cannock and Stafford, something which needs to be reinstated today. Most local trains south of Rugeley were worked by LNWR steam rail motors. Introduced in 1908, these vehicles made the service much more economic to operate. As a note under 1911 in Charles Clinker's 1954 "Chronology" explains – *"An analysis of the working costs of LNW steam rail motor cars showed that the receipts per mile in the Walsall, Rugeley and Lichfield area were 1/8d (8p), and expenses sixpence-farthing (2.75p), the highest and lowest figure respectively in the whole system"*. They were also victims of their own success, overcrowding causing replacement by conventional trains in 1913. Birchills had a pathetic service and Landywood Halt (opened 1908) is only mentioned in the footnote. Both were closed on New Year's Day, 1916.

A LNWR rail motor heads south across Cannock Chase, sometime between 1908-13. *(F.W.Shuttleworth collection)*

Table 262 BIRMINGHAM, SUTTON PARK, and WALSALL

Miles		Week Days a.m		a.m		p.m	p.m		p.m	p.m		Sundays p.m	p.m	p.m	p.m	p.m	p.m
												F	F	H	K	F	K
	Birmingham (NewSt)dep	7 18	..	8 13	..	1 10	5 35	..	6 35	8 5	..						
2	Saltley	7 24	..	8 19	..	1 16	5 41	..	6 41	8 12	..	..	..	..	..	..	..
5¼	Castle Bromwich....	7 30	..	8 25	..	1 22	5 47	..	6 47	8 19	..	..	..	..	..	..	..
8¾	Penns, for Walmley....	7 37	..	8 32	..	1 29	5 54	..	6 54	..	..	..	..	..	..	..	..
10	Sutton Park....	7 44	..	8 38	..	1 35	6 0	..	7 0	8 29	..	3 30	4 30	7 0	7 30	8 30	9 30
13¼	Streetly	7 52	..	8 44	..	1 41	6 6	..	7 6	8 35	..	3 36	4 36	7 6	7 36	8 36	9 36
15¾	Aldridge	7 58	..	8 50	..	1 47	6 12	..	7 12	8 41	..	3 42	4 42	7 12	7 42	8 42	9 42
17½	Walsall .... arr	8 4	..	8 56	..	1 53	6 18	..	7 18	8 47	..	3 49	4 49	7 19	7 49	8 49	9 51

Miles		Week Days a.m		a.m		p.m		p.m		p.m		Sundays p.m	p.m	p.m	p.m	p.m	
	Walsall.... dep	7 0	..	8 10	..	1 36	..	5 43	..	6 40	..	3 0	4 0	5 0	8 0	9 0	..
1¾	Aldridge	7 9	..	8 17	..	1 43	..	5 50	..	6 47	..	3 8	4 8	5 8	8 8	9 8	..
4¼	Streetly	7 15	..	8 22	..	1 48	..	5 55	..	6 52	..	3 13	4 13	5 13	8 13	9 13	..
7½	Sutton Park....	7 23	..	8 27	..	1 55	..	6 3	..	6 57	..	3 18	4 18	5 18	8 18	9 18	..
8¾	Penns, for Walmley....	7 31	..	8 33	..	2 3	..	6 12	..	7 3	..	F	F	F	F	K	..
12¼	Castle Bromwich....	7 37	..	8 39	..	2 9	..	6 20	..	7 12	..	..	..	..	..	..	..
15¼	Saltley	7 45	..	8 46	..	2 15	..	6 28	..	7 21	..	..	..	..	..	..	..
17½	Birmingham (NewSt)arr	7 51	..	8 52	..	2 22	..	6 35	..	7 29	..	..	..	..	..	..	..

F Runs from 28th May to 27th August inclusive
H Runs on 13th, 20th, and 27th August only
K Runs from 28th May to 6th August inclusive

For
OTHER TRAINS
between Birmingham and Castle Bromwich, see Tables 210 and 227

The LMS made drastic cutbacks to the passenger service on the Sutton Park line during the Second World War from which it never recovered. The table shown is for summer 1944. By this time the summer Sunday trains linking Walsall with Sutton Park had begun, a brief but useful means of escape from the arduous wartime working conditions. These trains continued until the summer of 1964 and this was the only regular interval service ever to operate over the line.

FOOTBALL ASSOCIATION — CUP FINAL

AT WEMBLEY STADIUM

WOLVERHAMPTON WANDERERS

VERSUS

BLACKBURN ROVERS

SATURDAY, 7th MAY, 1960

Train Number 718   To EUSTON

OUTWARD		am.	RETURN FARES s. d.
RUGELEY TOWN	dep.	6†50	
HEDNESFORD	"	7† 4	26 9
CANNOCK	"	7† 8	
WYRLEY and Cheslyn Hay	"	7†17	
BLOXWICH	"	7†25	26 0
WALSALL	"	7 40	25 6
EUSTON	arr.	10 40	

RETURN		night	12 1
EUSTON	dep.		
WALSALL	arr.		2 50
BLOXWICH	"		3† 2
WYRLEY and Cheslyn Hay	"		3† 9
CANNOCK	"		3†13
HEDNESFORD	"		3†23
RUGELEY TOWN	"		3†35

† Change at Walsall.

The 1960 Cup Final was won 3-0 by Wolves. From the Wolverhampton area there were 17 special trains – to Wembley Central (4), Wembley Hill (2), Euston (6) and Paddington (5). Details of train 718 are shown. What can only be imagined – after the victory of their team and a night's celebrations in the West End – is the state of some supporters as they emerged from their connecting dmu at stations along the Rugeley line after three o'clock on the Sunday morning.

SUNDAY 29th JUNE

★ DIESEL TRAIN TRIP ★

To ALTON TOWERS

FROM		DEPARTURE TIMES	RETURN FARES Second Class	ARRIVAL TIMES On Return
		am.	s.d.	pm.
WOLVERHAMPTON High Level	...	10 20	7/6	8 50
WILLENHALL	...	10 30	7/6	8 40
DARLASTON	...	10 35	7/-	8 35
WALSALL	...	10 45	6/6	8 25
PELSALL	...	10 55	6/6	8 20
BROWNHILLS	...	11 0	6/-	8 15
HAMMERWICH	...	11 5	5/6	8 10
LICHFIELD City	...	11 10	5/6	8 0
ALREWAS	...	11 25	5/-	7 50
		pm.		
ALTON TOWERS	... arr.	12 10		
Return same day at		pm.		
		7 0		H.D.

Admission tickets to the Towers—Adults 2/-, Children 1/- can be obtained at Wolverhampton and Walsall when booking Rail tickets.

A fifteen page leaflet was necessary to advertise all the area's excursion trains for just three Sundays in June 1958. Almost seven hours sampling the delights of Alton Towers for just 42p return from Walsall sounds like a bargain. However, there were no white knuckle rides then, just a beautiful garden, fairground rides and a model railway. The train would have been routed via Burton and Uttoxeter, where the North Staffs branch to Leek, via Alton, diverged.

WALSALL AT BIRMINGHAM

These photographs show Birmingham New Street during the transition from steam to diesel traction. All feature Walsall line trains, except for the last one, where the concrete bunker of the new station can be seen emerging from the ruins of the old.

This picture captures the shabby rundown image of the railway at a time when fewer than 4% of commuters in the West Midlands used the train. Local diesel services had begun in 1956 and, judging by this photograph, that was not before time. Ivatt 2-6-0 Class 2, No.46454 leaks smoke and steam into the dingy surroundings of Platform 2 at New Street as it forms the 4.17pm to Walsall, Lichfield and Burton-upon-Trent on 8th February 1958. *(Michael Mensing)*

Birmingham New Street. The roof over the London North Western side of the station was severely damaged in air raids during the Second World War. It was dismantled, and temporary roofs over the LNW platforms were erected in 1948. These lasted until the station was completely rebuilt in the 1960s. In the interim, much of the station area remained open to the sky, for the first and last time in its history. The Queen's Hotel survived the war and provides the cliff in the background of this shot. Ex-LMS Stanier Class 4 2-6-4 tank, No.42560 has just arrived at Platform 3 with the 07.17 from Rugeley Trent Valley on Good Friday, 4th April 1958. *(Michael Mensing)*

A Park Royal dmu stands empty at New Street's Platform 9, on the Midland side of the station, 7 pm on 12th June 1958, having arrived with the last train of the day from Walsall via the Sutton Park line. New Street No.4 Signal Box, featured here, was a one-man cabin of 73 levers controlling the west end of the Midland side of the station. It possessed some colour lights installed in 1952. All its signals controlling access to and from the main lines at the west end were slotted with their equivalents in No.5 Box, a 153 lever three-man cabin, the biggest at New Street, responsible for all movements into and out of the station over the Wolverhampton and West Suburban lines. *(Michael Mensing)*

A 2 car Metro Cammel dmu at the Derby end of Platform 9, New Street, forms the 6.44pm to Walsall via Penns, the last train of the day over the Sutton Park Line, 1st July 1961. This set was in the original livery for these units, where the overall green was enlivened by a third cream line, curving up from above the cab end whiskers to run along the sides, parallel with the base of the window vents. Few passengers must have noticed this detail; they would have welcomed an improved service. However, the replacement diesels were no more frequent than Sutton Park steam had been, and the opportunity to revive its passenger service when they were introduced was lost. *(Michael Mensing)*

A well loaded two car Park Royal dmu gets a clear road out of New Street from a diminutive signal at the Wolverhampton end of Platform 5. This was the 5.24pm to Walsall via the Soho Loop on 24th September 1959.

(Michael Mensing)

Birmingham New Street in transition, 29th September 1965. The Victorian overall roofs which had once covered the station where about to be replaced by a suffocating concrete blanket. In the meantime, the platforms were basking all too briefly in the sunlight. There is a wealth of detail here which repays close inspection with a magnifying glass. Much of the station is a building site. Work began on the Midland side, to the right, and the old LNWR platforms and the Queen's Hotel are still intact. Queen's Drive has gone but a stub of the old footbridge survives. The right of way was maintained throughout rebuilding and is marked by the fence across the concrete raft. The unidentified 'Peak' diesel will depart over the West Suburban line towards Bristol. The New Street-Euston service virtually ceased to exist during rebuilding, but the Snow Hill-Paddington trains were augmented. Trains from Walsall via Sutton Park no longer ran, although they had briefly used New Street's first rebuilt platforms just before withdrawal. The new signal box was not commissioned until 1966 (it became a listed building in 1995), so Box Number 1 with 63 levers - some of which worked colour lights dating back to 1924 - was still functioning. It can be seen near the base of the Rotunda. The spire belongs to St.Martin's in the Bull Ring, the centre of Birmingham in the Middle Ages.

(courtesy of Central Trains)

71

CHAPTER SIX : BESCOT AND RYECROFT

(Bescot - Steam, Yard and Depot : Ryecroft and Memories)

Bescot - Steam ....

Bescot's large marshalling yard and engine shed opened in 1892. The shed, designed for 32 locos, had eight 200 foot long roads, all with inspection pits beneath. There was a 42 foot turntable nearby and a coaling stage topped by a 65,000 gallon water tank about 200 yards down the yard. This was LNWR Shed Number 6 and, thanks to the continued increase in freight traffic, it soon became overcrowded, with an allocation of 63 locos in 1912, rising to 81 in 1923. With the birth of the LMS that year, the shed code was changed to 3A, one by which it has been known ever since, despite the official changes to 21B in 1960 and 2F in 1963. A landmark during steam days was the mechanical coaling plant, built by Wellman Smith Owen in 1936, which had a capacity of only 75 tons. The sights and sounds of this machine, as a laden truck was lifted into its bowels, or as coal was disgorged into a waiting loco's tender, were familiar to the boys clustered on the platform and footbridge at the station, a short distance away. A vacuum operated 60 foot turntable replaced the original in 1936 and the shed received a new louvred roof during the winter of 1949/50.

The Ian Allan shed book for April 1952 shows an allocation of 66 locomotives, of which 10 were mixed traffic Ivatt 2-6-0s or 4-6-0s. The rest were freight locos, ranging in size and power from 2F and 3F ex-Midland 0-6-0s (5 locos) to 7F Super Ds (23) and ex-LMS 8F 2-8-0s (26). The balance consisted of two diesel shunters, one for each side of the yard. By 1954, with 70 locos, the classes represented had spread to include 'Crabs' and Stanier Black 5s. A new diesel depot was constructed near the steam shed, which closed on 28th March 1966, although its shell still stands.

Bescot was known for its large number of Super Ds, heavy 0-8-0 freight locos built to the design of Charles John Bowen-Cooke of the LNWR and introduced in 1912. Some lingered here until 1964, the last ex-London & North Western locos on British Railways. Ray Churchill worked out of Bescot firing these locos during the last ten years of their lives. All lines out of Bescot, except the up Grand Junction, are on a rising gradient. The toughest work for a Super D was the 'Wichnor job' over the South Staffs line to Lichfield and beyond, because of the gradient. Southbound trains returning to Bescot were also faced with a long climb, from Brookhay, north of Lichfield, to the summit at Brownhills. The Super D was not the easiest locomotive to fire because it had a flat firebox and wide thick firebars with narrow air gaps. The fire had to be spread thinly and evenly all round the box, almost in th shape of a saucer, to ensure a decent head of steam. When on a D for the first time, the fireman almost invariably drew back the shovel to swing it into the firebox, cracking his knuckles on either the tender brake wheel or the water scoop wheel handle, depending on which side of the cab he was standing. This would happen several more times before he became accustomed to the cab layout. Although unforgiving to an indifferent or inexperienced fireman it was a very strong engine. It sat hard on the rails because of the eight driving wheels - there were no leading bogies or trailing wheels to dissipate the traction or lessen the grip. "You could hang the weight on behind a Super D", said Ray. It had a very distinctive sound, two heavy beats followed by two lighter beats, due to the Joy valve gear which used no eccentrics. The valve movements were derived from levers fastened to th connecting rods. Any speed in excess of 30mph resulted in 'hunting'.

The last surviving members of the class all had tender cabs. This was some protection from the weather when travelling tender first but it was a nuisance when disposing of the engine on shed, because the fireman had to paddle the fire out with a long shovel and the back of the cab used to get in the way and "they did become a bit of a nightmare in that respect". In the summer they were very hot because the back head had no cladding and the heat given off, coupled with the heat off the tender cab from the sun, was enough to cook the train crew.

Enginemen working in Bescot's disposing link had the task of cleaning, coaling, watering and generally preparing locos for their next turn of duty. This was where they discovered how awkward the Super Ds could be to get started, especially if steam pressure was low and the boiler was full, because they tended to run away. They had a parallel boiler and a distinctive dome for collecting steam. Even with a full boiler, steam pressure after disposal might hav dropped down to just 50lbs/sq.in. The Super Ds had total vacuum braking and 50lbs. was not sufficient pressure to create enough vacuum to get the brake off, so train crews used to loose off the reservoirs so that there was no brake at all and take them down to the shed. One track in the disposal area, the back ash pit road, had a slight gradient on a tight curve, and on that line in particular, they needed all the regulator, the whole throttle, at this low pressure in order to move. Once under way the regulator would shut off, but with a large amount of water in the boiler they tended to 'take off' and the fireman would have to react promptly with the reversing wheel and wind it back - if he could. If it had earlier been wound forward hard it could lock in that position. It was then a case of hitting the reversing wheel hard with the coal peck. Having been released by this low-tech method, the wheel was wound back rapidly until the loco slowed down. Sometimes it would lock the other way and the Super D would stop and then start going backwards.

One of the more memorable Super D trips for Ray Churchill was the daily relief freight from Bescot to Washwood Heath via the Sutton Park line. Once up the incline from Ryecroft and past the summit through Aldridge, skilled drivers would feel confident enough to cut the brake out. Shutting off the brake valve would save water and on a Super D it was known as 'screwing out the rose' on account of the rose-like pattern on the brake reservoir valve wheel. The train, with its long rake of empty mineral wagons, would then go gently down the grade without brakes, from the second summit at Streetly through Sutton Park and Penns, the valve only screwed back in for the curve at Park Lane Junction. As the wagons had no brakes which could be controlled from the loco cab, and as the brake in the guards van was of doubtful value in such circumstances, the train was not that far removed from being an unguided missile, albeit a slow moving one. The wagons were delivered to Washwood Heath, and then the light engine ran tender first to Water Orton, to pick up a train of heavy steel slab to be delivered, via Sutton Park and

A good close up shot of a Super D in original condition, with smaller chimney and rounded firebox. Believed to have been taken at Bescot, about 1925. These locos were then Class 6, with a boiler pressure of 160lb/sq.inch. They became Class 7 when upgraded with 175lb boilers. *(Don Powell collection)*

Super D No.49106 on shunting duty at the former Midland station at Willenhall (Stafford Street), c.1960. *(Ray Churchill)*

A train of northbound empties trundles onto the Walsall line at Bescot, 17th March 1962. The star beneath the cabside number (48256), indicates that this loco had finely balanced wheels and was passed for faster running (up to 60mph) with fitted freight trains. One of Bescot's stud of 'Starred 8s' would sometimes deputise for a Black 5 on the fast fitted freight to London (Camden).   *(Michael Mensing)*

the Midland avoiding line at Ryecroft, to Ductile Steel at Willenhall. Such a trip would need a loco in good order but towards the end of the Super D's working lives their front ends were often in very poor condition and it was difficult to see the road ahead, as there seemed to be more steam outside the boiler than in!

The ex-LMS Class 8F heavy freight 2-8-0 locomotives were the mainstay of goods traffic on the South Staffs line for several years before the end of steam. Coming south from Lichfield a heavy 'Wichnor freight' could be held at the City station if the line was busy. After a check at Lichfield it was usual practice to hammer the train as hard as possible and on past Anglesey Sidings in order not to stall on the gradient in Pipe Hill Cutting, Brownhills. Around 1960 a bonus system was introduced which meant, essentially, that the faster a job was completed the more the train crew would be paid. A Class 8, in the hands of a good driver, could be coaxed into behaving like an express, and this often happened at Anglesey at the time. A high earning favourite with the men was a double trip to Wichnor in one shift. The second trip finished at Windsor Street Goods, Aston, with gas coal in 16 ton mineral wagons. The maximum number of such wagons allowed into Windsor Street on any one train was 34. As most mineral trains extended to about 50 wagons, this train was - in comparison -short, fast and profitable for men lucky enough to work it.

Yard ....
Bescot Marshalling Yard was upgraded as part of British Railways' Modernisation Plan of 1955. Major reconstruction was completed in 1965. There were reception and sorting sidings in the up yard, while the larger down yard also had such sidings, plus local sorting and storage sidings. A new tower signalbox was opened in the down yard. New humps, together with the Dowty Automatic Wagon Handling System, speeded up the process of marshalling the down yard's trains. However, the Dowty system was designed for traditional short-wheelbase wagons, which were becoming obsolete. It proved not to be adaptable to the larger rolling stock of the 1970s, so it was removed about 1982.

Electrification of the West Coast Main Line between Euston - Birmingham - Manchester/Liverpool was completed in 1967. It included lines mainly or exclusively used by freight, such as Bescot - Wolverhampton, Pleck Junction - Darlaston Junction, Aston - Stechford and the Soho Loop. Much of Bescot Yard was also wired. Had there been a continous rolling programme of electrification in Britain - as has happened in most European countries - most main lines would now be under the wires, with a high proportion of freight trains hauled by electric locomotives. Gaps between electrified parts of what was once our rail network are always inconvenient and often short, eg; Walsall - Rugeley. To avoid the trouble and expense of changing traction, large diesel mileages are run under the wires. Nowadays, not a single regular working into or out of Bescot Yard is diagrammed for electric traction! The only electric freight train passing through is the Willesdan to Coatbridge Freightliner, which can be seen heading north at around 16.30 each weekday.

Bescot remains busy, one of the very few large yards of the 1960s that has not been either closed or severely downgraded. The current layout, which has been modified since 1965, is shown in the accompanying diagram. The down yard consists of

Bescot Yard 1996

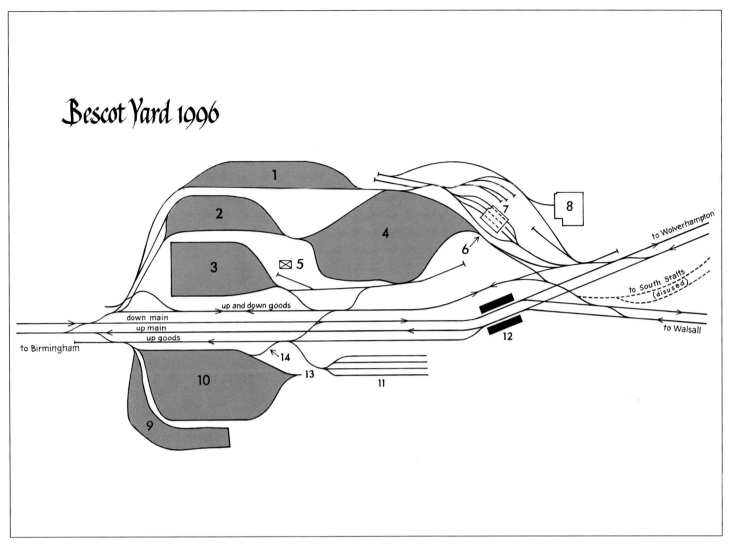

7 storage sidings (1) primarily used for the storage of merry-go-round wagons for local collieries, 7 up and down reception sidings (2), 10 local sorting sidings (3) and 20 sorting sidings (4). Most shunting activity takes place at the north end of the down yard, where there is a shunting loco on duty twenty-four hours per day. Other prominent features are the down tower signalbox (5) which has two panels - one each for Railtrack and Transrail - linked to Walsall power box, the single lead into/out of the yard (6), the traction maintenance depot (7) and the shell of the steam shed (8). Nowadays, the down yard accommodates down and up trains, which are normally held in the down sorting sidings, which they enter or leave via the down tower hump (5A).

The main components of the former up yard are 6 local sorting sidings (9), 16 sorting sidings (10) and the former reception sidings (11). The bulk of the sorting sidings are used by the civil engineer's department, with wagons containing ballast, rails, sleepers and track maintenance equipment. The sidings at (11) were used for storing locos and connected to the main line by a lead line running behind the station (12). The lead line was removed in 1982. Open access meant there was a problem with vandalism and locos have been stored more securely at (3) since 1994, although stored wagons are still held at (11). The link to the sorting sidings at (13) was removed in 1994 to save renewing a pair of hand points. The link at (14), known as the bottom slip, dates from the 1965 modernisation and is worked from the points box, which is still manned. The station, now known as Bescot Stadium, is equipped with wide platforms to handle match day crowds in safety. A useful bi-directional goods line runs between the station and the down yard. On one occasion early in 1996 the points at the north end failed when they were set for this line. As it does not have a platform face the next emu from Birmingham had to continue to Walsall, where Bescot passengers were assured that the train would stop at their station on its return journey.

A large proportion of the freight at Bescot consists of power station coal. Much of this is sourced from Daw Mill and several Nottinghamshire pits, plus Silverdale and Mid-Cannock opencast. It is despatched to Ironbridge and Rugeley power stations. This traffic is heaviest during the winter, which also sees flows of imported coal through the yard. During the winter of 1995/6 there were up to four trains per day from Avonmouth to Ironbridge. Other important flows, apart from the engineers trains, are quarry ballast and china clay. Bescot is one of two main intermediate nodes on Transrail's Enterprise network. In essence the Enterprise trains run to a high speed time-table, convey several different traffics, and are re-marshalled en route, as happens at Bescot. They are a positive answer to the killing off of the Speedlink network, a vigorous acknowledgement that freight in less-than-trainload quantities is viable. For example, there used to be a daily Newport - Bescot metal products train. From 23rd September 1995 it became the Swansea - Warrington Enterprise, a much more versatile beast which now conveys up to five different traffics. The Willesden - Mossend Enterprise service (6S44) conveys steel coils from Sheerness to Bescot, from where they are tripped to Brierley Hill Steel Terminal. The southbound train (6M27) carries carbon dioxide tanks for Coleshill Distillers' private siding.

Bescot in the 1920s. A short mixed freight heads onto the Grand Junction line. It is hauled by a Webb coal engine, a class of about 200 locos which immediately pre-dated the 'Cauliflowers'. They had wooden buffer beams and tender frames and were very economical to build and operate. A familiar one at Bescot was given the LMS number 28199. Various unidentified locos are stabled in the background, on what is still very much a green field site, although West Bromwich Corporation's large sewage farm at Friar Park lurks menacingly downwind, just beyond the rising ground. The most striking feature of this photograph is the immaculate condition of the track, Walsall line to the left and the curve up to the South Staffs in the centre. *(Bob Lane collection)*

There were two tank versions of the Super D, known as D tanks. They were used mainly for shunting and local freight trips. Here 7885 is seen shunting at Bescot, about 1938. The rear sand box was useful when it was working bunker first. With eight small driving wheels this loco clung tenaciously to the track. (The other version had a 0-8-4 wheel arrangement). *(F.W. Shuttleworth)*

"Royal Scot" 42120 "Royal Inniskilling Fusilier" at the rear of Bescot's coaling plant, having worked a football special from London to Witton for the Villa Park semi-final of the FA Cup, 1956. In the match, Manchester City defeated Tottenham Hotspur by the only goal.

(Jack Haddock)

A row of condemned engines at Bescot, Super D No.49045 to the fore, about 1960. Electrification of the West Coast Main Line had begun and the gallows seen here, complete with 'wiring', was a reminder to train crews of the new hazard they would face out on the line.

(Jack Haddock)

"John H.Carless V.C.", No.31 107, is seen passing Bescot, its home depot, on 27th October 1993.

Stephen Widdowson)

and Depot

Essential to the smooth running of the area's freight traffic is Bescot Traction Maintenance Depot (TMD), owned by Transrail. It has three through roads and a refuelling road to one side. The TMD is part of Transrail's 'Fleet Engineers South', which has its headquarters in Cardiff. The depot (spring 1996) had an allocation of 52 locomotives, consisting of classes 08, 09, 20, 31, 37. Normally this fleet has an 85% availability. The 08 shunters are dispersed over a wide area - one within Bescot yard, one each at Wolverhampton Steel Terminal, Oxley Carriage Sidings and Rugby. Work for such locos is contracting; during 1996 Bescot 08s were withdrawn from the yards at Bletchley and Northampton and the merry-go-round depot at Burton. The second yard shunter was withdrawn from Bescot itself.

The depot can undertake anything from light repairs to heavy E examinations. Engine components, compressors, traction motors and wheel sets can all be changed here. The depot is staffed 7 days a week, 24 hours per day, providing employment for 35 people. Because neighbouring Transrail depots are at Wigan and Cardiff, Bescot is developing a role as an administrative centre and components store for a large area, from Chester down to Bletchley.

I was told by Andrew Skinner, Depot Engineer, that I had visited on an average day, 24th May 1996. A variety of locos was to be seen near the TMD. A Dutch-liveried Class 37 was in company with 20 075 "Sir William Cook" in British Telecom livery, 31 319 based at Wigan Springs in Trainload Coal livery, 08 625, 08 683, 08 519 in black livery, 31 524 in Dutch livery, 37 671 based at St.Blazey and 56 092.

There was a need to expand the depot in the mid-1980s, so a new fuel road (Road 1) was built at the side, releasing the old one (Road 2) within the depot. For a routine service check a loco is within the depot for about one and a half hours. Roads 3 and 4 are used for major examinations and heavy work. Equipment includes a hoist and four-point lifting jacks with a total lift capacity of 100 tonnes, able to raise a loco clear of its bogies. Lastly, the depot stores hold components and parts ranging up to cylinder heads, springs, pistons - and buffers.

The tradition of servicing a busy yard and a varied fleet of freight locomotives at Bescot, which goes back over a hundred years, is still being maintained with enthusiasm and dedication today.

"The best laid schemes of mice and men ...." A view looking south towards Ryecroft, taken on 24th July 1962. The photographer was standing on the bridge carrying the Midland avoiding line, where it overlooks the Lichfield line. The huge expanse of well-prepared nothing is the site for the new electric shed, intended to house the emus that were to operate from Walsall to Birmingham, Rugeley and Lichfield.

(courtesy of Railtrack)

Ryecroft and Memories

The opening date of Ryecroft is uncertain, but it was authorised in October 1877, to replace the earlier South Staffs shed, which was a little to the south. LNWR shed No.9, it became 3C, a sub-shed of Bescot (3A) in 1935, 21F in 1960 and 2G in 1963. It had twelve roads, all with pits, and a capacity of 48 locos - in other words, it was larger than the more famous Bescot shed. There was no turntable until 1933, when a 60 foot vacuum operated table was provided. The coaling plant, installed in 1937, was slow, needing up to 30 minutes to load a loco which had an empty tender. The Midland Railway, with its Wolverhampton and Sutton Park lines, had its own small shed at Walsall, near the Wednesbury Road bridge. This closed in 1925 and its 14 locos were relocated to Ryecroft.

The April 1952 Ian Allan shed book lists 54 engines at Ryecroft - 28 freight, 4 passenger and 22 mixed traffic. They included 13 Super Ds and 3 ex-Midland 4-4-0 2P passenger engines. Seventeen of the mixed traffic locos were tank engines used on local push-pull trains.

Ryecroft's hopes were to be unfulfilled. A new shed roof had been planned in 1948 but nothing was done until 1956, by which time it was decided that it would become a diesel depot. Steam ceased here in June 1958 and the remaining locos were sent to Bescot (freight) or Aston (passenger). With an allocation of new diesel multiple units the future looked bright and it seemed to be getting brighter. During the first half of 1962 land to the north was prepared for the site of a new shed to house electric multiple units which, it was intended, would operate services to Birmingham, Rugeley and Lichfield. Clearances were improved on the Cannock line ready for the expected catenary. The section between Rugeley Trent Valley and Rugeley Town was wired and energised – it remains so. There were even plans to stable a few

electric locomotives here to work freight trains and a daily passenger train between Walsall and Euston. Mill Lane separated the new electric area from the rest of the shed, so the BR Board bought its right of way to convert it into an access road. Alas, from out of the murk there rose forth a Beeching, which decreed that only the Birmingham line was to be electrified and all other local services from Walsall were to be closed. When this happened, in January 1965, the need for any kind of facility at Ryecroft ceased. The empty shell stood lifeless until it was demolished in 1968. What of the memories of some of the men who worked there?

Tom King was born in Walsall in 1898. He began work at Ryecroft in 1924, but his railway memories go back to 1916. He was employed by the Midland Railway at Derby, which suffered an air raid, killing five railwaymen, in the early evening of 31st January. A force of seven Zeppelins dropped bombs on the city, after which they headed for Birmingham, navigating by prominent physical features, which often meant the railway lines. At about 8pm one of them appeared over Walsall, which presented an easy target because lighting restrictions were not being observed. Among the casualties was Mrs.S.M.Slater, Mayoress of Walsall, hit by schrapnel from a bomb which fell in Bradford Place, near the station. She had been travelling in a passing tramcar and died of her wounds on 20th February. It was reckoned at the time that this lone Zeppelin became separated from the others when, in observing the railway lines, its navigator mis-read Park Lane Junction south of Water Orton, and followed the Sutton Park line to its target.

On the Saturday after Christmas 1928, Tom fired the last train from Walsall to Rugeley. It was virtually empty because of thick lying snow. At Hednesford he looked within the compartments.

Had they all been empty the train would have turned back but in one a man was stretched out naked and drunk, with a cockerel he had bought at market perched on the rack. He told Tom, "I've put them in the wardrobe" having thrown his clothes out of the window somewhere along the line. The Hednesford shunter knew him and said he would see to him. He was found some old clothes, plus Tom's overalls, his shoes were retrieved from under the seat and he was escorted home. On the return journey, his clothes were easily spotted in the snow between Bloxwich and Ryecroft. A Walsall porter parcelled them up and sent them on to Hednesford. On this occasion Tom's driver was Ted 'Toffee' Everton, a man with a legendary capacity for beer, who seemed incapable of getting drunk. He gave his address as 11and three-quarters Intown Row, next to the army barracks in Whittimere Street, where he 'moonlighted' as caretaker, having charge of the barracks bar. He had served with the South Staffordshire Regiment in the First World War and always attended their annual dinner. At this event in 1930 one of the guests was John Waddington, Shed Superintendent at Ryecroft. After the dinner Ted was closely observed by his boss with growing disbelief, as he consumed numerous pints of ale. Waddington left at about 1am, knowing that Ted was due on duty at 6am. He rose early, only to see Ted arrive for work at 5.50am, completely sober. When asked what his limit was for drinking ale, Ted replied, *"I am sorry sir, I don't know, for I have neither the time nor money to put it to the test"*, before disappearing in the direction of the Webb tank that was rostered for him. When working the midday local train from Walsall to Derby, he had an arrangement with the Station Hotel at Pelsall. On the approach from Heath End he sounded a special code on the whistle, which alerted the landlord to pull a pint of best bitter and place it on the bar, handle towards the door. The one minute's booked stop at Pelsall would be sufficient for 'Toffee' Everton to run across the road, consume his beer and be back on the footplate ready to depart.

George Loftus began his railway career at Ryecroft as a 17 year old in 1935. During the ten years he was there he graduated from cleaner to passed cleaner (allowed to fire), to fireman and passed fireman (allowed to drive). He worked on a variety of lines, including the Leighswood branch and other little known byways such as a branch off the Norton Junction - Cannock line known as the Conduit. Working the Dudley Dasher he knew its two carriages as 'Gert & Daisy' after popular radio comediennes. Two members of the then new "Jubilee" Class were allocated to Ryecroft, 5603 "Solomon Islands" and 5604 "Ceylon". Such locos were used for summer excursions from Walsall to Blackpool, Llandudno and Weston-super-Mare, which all regularly loaded to fourteen carriages.

A particularly happy period was the eighteen months during which he fired the ex-Midland 4-4-0 loco rostered to haul the Engineer's train, which was based at Walsall. This train consisted of just the Engineer's saloon and, with coach and loco kept in immaculate condition, people sometimes mistook it for a royal train. He was still on this duty at the outbreak of war. The Engineer's authority to inspect and close lines forthwith if need be took on a new significance with the advent of air raid damage.

The war years are remembered by George without the almost fond nostalgia that clouds some peoples memories. At night, especially in summer, working on the footplate was hot and oppressive because of the tarpaulin over the cab, necessary to dim the glow from the firebox. Once George was firing a Walsall train waiting to leave New Street when bombs began falling on the station. Despite the mayhem the signalmen and station staff *"got us away as quickly as they could"*. It soon became obvious to railwaymen working into New Street that after an air raid there would be numbers of ghoulish people travelling into the city 'just

Railwaymen pose on a Super D at Ryecroft 1936, George Loftus upper right. *(George Loftus collection)*

to have a look'. Train crews would receive warning from signalmen of possible damage to the line and they would proceed gingerly in the thick blackness at no more than 15 mph, *"because you never knew if the track was there or not"*.

There was a long goods loop at Bromford Bridge, used by trains from the Derby and Sutton Park lines. This was a permissive line, in other words, normal signalling rules did not apply and trains could queue in it nose to tail. Up to six trains would gather and, with the difficulties of wartime transport, it was not unknown for George and his mate to relieve a crew on one train only to find at the end of their shift that they were relieved in turn without having moved! Employment on the railway was a reserved occupation, exempt from military service. As proof of their occupation LMS footplatemen were issued with small blue embossed enamel badges, a loco at the top and 'LMS' at the base, separated by a red stripe inscribed 'Railway Service'.

Ryecroft crews regularly worked troop trains from Lichfield as far as Cheltenham, and from Liverpool to the Midlands. The least attractive 'troop' train was the last departure from Walsall on Saturdays, full of RAF personnel returning to Brindley Heath. Many of the men were drunk, some travelled on the luggage racks, some urinated out of the open doors of the moving train and others were accompanied by girls who came along ' for the ride' - amongst other things.

Ex-Midland Railway 4-4-0 No.40646 at Bescot. One of a large class of 4-4-0 passenger locos built to the design of Samuel Johnson in 1900. Except for the absence of outside cylinders, these handsome 'simple' engines were similar in appearance to the more powerful 'Midland Compounds', which dated from 1902. This was the Walsall engineer's locomotive, consequently it always appeared smart - even the inside front of the cab was blacked - seen here some time after its sixtieth birthday.   *(Ray Churchill)*

The war years, of course, meant extra hard work for everyone. If there was nobody available to relieve a driver or fireman at the end of a long shift he just had to carry on. George Loftus was once booked to fire a train from Walsall to Crewe. On arrival there was nobody to relieve him, so he continued to Carlisle, by which time he had shifted seven tons of coal and needed to be carried from the footplate.

Ken Roberts began his career at Ryecroft, as a passed cleaner and fireman, just after the second World War. Everything about the place seemed rundown. The shed was gaslit, often with broken mantles; the only electricity was on some pumps used for boiler cleaning. The toilets were earth closets, emptied every night - it was rumoured - into the recently redundant air raid shelters. The turntable was worked by the loco's vacuum brake, but it was temperamental. Cleaners and others were often enlisted to help turn it manually. For the hardest part, getting it started, pinch bars were used. With a hard pressed cleaning gang, it often seemed the only thing cleaned was the loco number. They worked in the heat, ashes and dirt without the benefit of gloves or face masks. Some repairs could be carried out at Ryecroft. If a steam loco needed its brick firebox arch replacing it was out of action for some time, because a week was needed to allow the old bricks to cool down sufficiently for them to be removed. As at most steam sheds there was a sand furnace. It was fed with 10 tons of sand at a time, which was dried by two fires underneath, kept burning the year round. In this way there was always a supply of dry sand for use by locos on slippery or greasy rails.

The winter of 1947 was very severe, needing the force of three Super Ds behind a snowplough to clear the Cannock line. The weather and tight coal rationing led to an outbreak of stealing, or 'coal jagging'. Some local people even took it from within the shed. A favourite place for such activity was south of Bloxwich station. Southbound coal trains would stop at the top of the descent to Ryecroft while the guard walked along pinning some wagon brakes down. In the dark it was impossible for him to keep an eye on the whole train, so jaggers would creep along, open truck doors and steal coal, their friends on hand to help them away with it.

A long slow job for Ryecroft crews was the overnight freight to Camden. It was unfitted, so rarely exceeded 30 mph, calling at Bodley's Sidings, Bescot, Stechford, Northampton and lesser places to pick up as required. The crew would have supper 'on the shovel', but if the fireman had earlier upset his driver, he could see his meal disappear into the fire as his 'mate' opened and shut the regulator smartly.

One Saturday morning, Ray had just reported for work when he heard a cry for help from his driver. He had been up on the loco filling the lubricators before coming down onto the front buffer beam. He was not wearing bicycle clips and caught his trouser leg on the lamp bracket - which was about 1 foot (30cm) long - with such force that it tipped him over and he broke his leg. He was never able to work on the footplate again. Another of Ken's regular drivers, Frank, never let anything bother him. One Saturday they took an excursion from Walsall to Rhyl. The first carriage was occupied by a group of yobs who leaned out of the windows and taunted them with foul language, in the station and on the move. *"Tek no notice"*, said Frank calmly. At Wolverhampton, as they came to rest alongside the water column he said, *"Fill the tank up me lad, and don't shut the lid"*. The abuse from the train continued unabated but at the water troughs beyond Stafford, Frank gave Ken a quick lesson in the use of the scoop, causing water to overflow and drench the train. *"Have a look"*, said Frank. Not a window was open. *"Told ya day I?"* he said chirpily.

Preparing a loco for the road was known as 'spotting' and sometimes one train crew was rostered to spend their entire shift spotting locos for eight other crews. This was boring work, but not as bad as hump shunting, which Ken confessed to hating. Even that had its compensations, because he came to appreciate the skill of the signalman, which he referred to as 'the bobby in the box' just as signalmen in th earliest days of railways were sometimes known as 'policemen'. When hump shunting took place at night, the box was in darkness. The signalman could see out better, but nothing at all within. He still had to operate levers quickly, often at opposite ends of the frame, and he seemed to know them by touch alone. By contrast, Ken's happiest memories were of goods trains over the Chase in the middle of clear starry nights, "so peaceful, you could be on another planet".

John Westwood began his railway career at Ryecroft with a batch of other 15 year olds straight from school, in August 1955. On the first day they were issued with scrapers, buckets filled with paraffin and a rag. They were told to scrape the muck off the loco wheels and wipe them over with paraffin to get rid of the residue. The lads were soon filthy and soaked with foul-smelling paraffin. After a few months of such work they went to Walsall station for an induction course, so that they could become passed cleaners. It was given by Inspector Harris and included lessons in the workings of steam locomotives. The acronym for the constituents of coal was NO CASH - Nitrogen Oxygen Carbon Ash Sulphur Hydrogen. There were working models of the three main types of valve gear - Joy, Walschaerts and Stephenson.

Having passed the course, John and the others were allocated to the disposing link, the lowest in the hierarchy of links at the shed. They were allowed an hour to dispose of each loco after its turn of duty was completed but if needs must, it could be done in a lot less time. On the day of the 1956 Cup Final no fewer than six locos were completed in an hour. Three were Class 2 tank engines with rocker grates, which could be done in 15 minutes in normal circumstances. Afterwards they went to watch television, only to see their team, Birmingham City, defeated 3-1 by Manchester City.

Some working practices would be considered too dangerous today. On a night freight over the South Staffs line, John's driver instructed him to jump from the moving train and run alongside to pin the wagon brakes down before the descent into Stourbridge. At 2am it was pitch black, with uneven ground strewn with unseen hazards. It would have been so easy to trip and fall under the wheels.

Leighswood Siding was "a roller coaster of a line", which crossed the canal with no ballast or decking on the bridge, just cross girders. It served the Atlas Brickworks and Barnett & Beddows. The elderly ex-Midland locos that worked the siding could be unpredictable at speed. When John was firing one on the Stour Valley at about 45 mph, he opened the firebox door and a huge tongue of flame lashed out and hit the tender, forcing him to hang over the side of the cab while his driver struggled to close the door. Another local fireman received permanent burns in a similar incident.

Like so many others who began what they thought was a long term railway career in the 1950s, John Westwood soon turned to other work. He transferred from Ryecroft to Monument Lane, where he noticed a line of ex-Midland Compounds assembled 'dead' on shed and was told they were going for scrap. He saw the new dmus and, realising that they did not need a fireman, left the railway and went into engineering.

Maurice Newman began work at Ryecroft in 1953, well able to observe the shed's changing fortunes. Frank Wood & Son of Derby began reconstruction in 1955. The roof was even rebuilt with smoke troughs which could be adjusted to allow for the escape of diesel exhaust fumes. In 1956 Wood's clerk of works warned train crews that once reconstruction was complete and the contract honoured, Ryecroft would be closed and demolished. They thought it was a sick joke and laughed him to scorn. Some dmus arrived, together with two diesel shunters, one for Norton Junction (D3021) and one spare (ex-LMS No.12056). There were still more than 40 steam locos here, including Super Ds, 1946-built Ivatt push-pull tanks and 46712, the last Webb tank engine. Rebuilding was completed in 1957 and the men briefly enjoyed such luxuries as a proper mess room and flush toilets. Rumours of closure surfaced again and this time they proved true. The shed closed to steam in June 1958, six months later than planned.

Ryecroft continued in use as a diesel shed and was initially home to all twenty of the two-car Park Royal dmu twin sets. Plans to close Ryecroft completely and accommodate all its dmus at Monument Lane were delayed until Walsall lost almost all its passenger services in 1965.

For many years the shed played host to the locomotives of the "Pines Express", without being directly involved in the running of this train. The "Pines" linked Manchester with Bournemouth and its normal route through the West Midlands was via Wolverhampton and the Stour Valley line to New Street, then south via Five Ways. On summer Saturdays during the 1950s it was routed via Walsall, where it had a booked passenger stop. From Wolverhampton it ran via the Grand Junction, Pleck Curve, Walsall and the Sutton Park line to New Street. The southbound train was worked from Manchester London Road (now Piccadilly) by Longsight men, who detached at Walsall and took their loco - normally a Black 5, sometimes the Caprotti version - to Bescot. While the train had been running south a Saltley crew brought another Black 5 light engine over the Park line to Ryecroft, where it would be turned on the shed's notorious table. Maurice Newman was at the shed on the day when the "Pines'" fireman failed to put the handbrake on and halfway round the loco rolled off the table, embedding its tender in the bank. The combined efforts of Super D 48907 and a Class 8 freight loco failed to pull it free, despite a length of steel rope and heavily sanded rails, so Bescot's steam crane had to be summoned. On less eventful Saturdays the "Pines" loco would drop down to Walsall and pick up its train of 12 well-filled carriages. It soon passed the shed as it took the Sutton Park line, working hard and unassisted up the initial 1:68 gradient, *"It made them cough"*, recalled Maurice. The crew was relieved at Bath Green Park (now a Sainsburys store), where a Southern Region loco took the train forward over the Somerset & Dorset line.

Typical duties for Ryecroft men were on Walsall's many push-pull trains and the shed banking engine. The push-pulls always pulled from Walsall to Wolverhampton, Dudley and Birmingham (via Bescot) and propelled to Lichfield, Rugeley and over the Sutton Park line. In the Sutton Bay, at the north end of Walsall's island platform 2/3, the loco was always at the buffer end, to prevent its smoke from choking the signalman in the notorious No.3 box.

The banking engine was needed to assist freight trains up from Ryecroft on the Birchills, Cannock and Sutton Park lines. During 1953 Bagnalls at Stafford were still building the final batch of Great Western designed Class 8400 pannier tanks for the Western Region. In those days, before artificially high track access charges, it was actually cheaper for rolling stock to be delivered by rail rather than road. The Bagnall engines were routed via Cannock and Dudley to Stourbridge. They stopped at Ryecroft for coal and water, then Ryecroft men took them on to Stourbridge. Somehow - Maurice remains suitably vague on the subject - when 8425 was passing through for delivery to Worcester, he and some colleagues persuaded the shed foreman to detain it for a week, during which they tested it to the full on banking duties - "marvellous!". The following week it was the turn of 8426, but after that there were no further unofficial running-in trials.

A site visit with John Westwood revealed the changes that have taken place since closure. The Birchills and Lichfield lines are gone, and the four tracks into Walsall have been reduced to two. The site is covered with scrub and silver birch trees, although the earth bank still covers the air raid shelter. Looking north from Mill Lane bridge, it is hard to detect where the ground was cleared for the electric shed. Closer to hand one of the yard lights still rusts quietly at the top of its wooden post.

LMS "Royal Scot" 4-6-0 No.6141 "The North Staffordshire Regiment" quenches its thirst at Ryecroft. It is believed that this loco had just worked the "Pines Express" on the first leg of its journey from Manchester (London Road), one summer Saturday in 1934. To the right, out of camera range, was the new (1933) sixty foot turntable, operated by the loco's vacuum brake. As the years progressed it became notoriously unreliable.

Rebuilding Ryecroft shed in 1955 with ex-Midland 2F No. 58123 amongst the girders and open sky.   *(Maurice Newman)*

A rare visitor to Walsall station, photographed in 1934, pauses at the north end of Platform 2.   The express passenger locomotive is a four-cylinder 4-6-0, known as a Class 8. There were only twenty engines in the class, originally built in 1908 at Horwich for the Lancashire & Yorkshire Railway. George Hughes, Chief Mechanical Engineer of that company, rebuilt them with superheaters and enlarged cylinders from December 1920. This was his last major work before the 'Lanky' amalgamated with the LNWR on New Year's Day 1922. This could have been the loco for the "Pines Express", although it did not normally use Platform 2.   *(Frank Ash)*

Sulzer Bo-Bo diesel-electric, 5239, heads past Ryecroft towards Walsall with a fitted freight on 16th May 1973. The train is coming off the Sutton Park line and Ryecroft's unique four way junction was still intact. The vacant plot between the Lichfield and Rugeley lines is the site of Ryecroft engine shed.   *(Michael Mensing)*

CHAPTER SEVEN : A JOURNEY OF DESPAIR AND HOPE

(The Day Before Yesterday : Black Monday : A Long Campaign :
Some Ways Forward)

The Day Before Yesterday

In 1950 steam still had a monopoly in the Walsall area. Most local trains were worked on the push-pull principle - but what exactly was a push-pull? It normally consisted of a tank locomotive and a pair of non-corridor coaches, one of which was fitted with a driving cab. There was no need for the loco to run round at each end of the journey; so perhaps we could say today that a push-pull combined the nostalgia of steam with the convenience of a diesel multiple unit! Both loco and stock had to be specially fitted, as best described by Harry Pratt, Driver Manager, who began his 45 year railway career in 1948 at Bushbury Shed, Wolverhampton, where he regularly fired on push-pull trains to Walsall and beyond:-

"The two coach train was coupled to the locomotive with a shackle, two vacuum pipes, heater pipe and bell signal cable. When it was propelled the locomotive was at the rear and the fireman all alone on the footplate. The driver sat in the cab of the leading coach, which had two vacuum valves, one for the vacuum controlled regulator valve on the outside of the locomotive smokebox and the other for applying the brake. As a means of communication the fireman received bell signals from the driver and he would open the regulator on the footplate, initially to a required setting and then, by winding the reversing gear, he set the valve cut-off at an efficient and economical position according to the speed and gradient. Because of the extra responsibility of working push-pull trains, the fireman had to be specially examined and passed out by the Footplate Inspector, which provided another step towards becoming a driver. On occasion, extra coaches were necessary to cope with passenger demand and the loco would be positioned in the middle of the train, with two coaches at each end. The fireman would be alone on the footplate when travelling in either direction."

Crews of push-pull trains worked reasonable hours, without the night work or awkward shifts often associated with freight traffic.

In March 1956 the Birmingham-Sutton Coldfield-Lichfield service was completely dieselised overnight. As the busiest local service in the Midlands it was the obvious choice. Its units operated out of Monument Lane, temporarily the biggest diesel shed in the country. Before the end of the same year dmus had begun to infiltrate Birmingham-Walsall-Rugeley line services, although the dates of photographs in this book with confirm an overlap between steam and diesel on the route. In November 1958 an hourly dmu service was introduced between Birmingham, Walsall and Rugeley Trent Valley. This meant seven extra trains during the day, and steam was confined to a few peak hour workings. The "Cannock Advertiser" commented *"These handy little trains, each equipped with toilet, will provide more and speedier services and are cleaner"*. The same year the Walsall-Dudley service was dieselised. It was regular interval after a fashion, hourly for part of the day, two-hourly during the afternoons. Also in November 1958, all Walsall-Wolverhampton trains were combined with Walsall-Lichfield trains which were extended to Burton-on-Trent. The service was not at regular intervals but this was an imaginative move and new travel opportunities were opened up. The Walsall - Lichfield line briefly enjoyed a faster and more frequent service than ever before. There were 10 trains southbound, 9 northbound. The Walsall - Lichfield day return fare was 2 shillings (10p). One casualty was the station at Pleck, which closed as the Wolverhampton - Burton service began.

Apart from the new diesels, the image of the railway at the time was not modern. Most stations had hardly changed since Victorian times and many were covered in the layers of grime left by recently departed steam locos. Almost all were in dire need of cleaning and painting. Promotion and marketing of local rail services was virtually unknown - a 'customer led' train service was an alien concept. At a time when car ownership was rising and most competing buses were cheaper and more frequent, this was a crucial weakness. In the early 1960s, the combination of a Minister of Transport, Ernest Marples, whose family was building its fortune on road construction, and a Chairman of British Railways, Richard Beeching, a chemist from ICI whose understanding of railways was slight, meant that local lines all over the country were ripe for slaughter. The Beeching Report, recommending closure of over 2,000 stations, was published in 1963 and little time was wasted in implementing it.

Black Monday

Notice of closure for the Walsall - Rugeley service was published in January 1964. A vigorous campaign against it was organised by the "Cannock Advertiser", with the support of the town's MP Jenny Lee (widow of Aneurin Bevan). The hearing took place in Walsall Town Hall in April, at which there were 246 written objections and 41 from people who appeared in person. Cannock Urban District Council, Cannock RDC and Rugeley UDC all objected on the grounds of hardship. An estimated 80,000 people would be deprived of a rail service, replacement buses would be slower and unable to cope easily with mothers with prams, people with luggage, etc. Such scenes were repeated in town halls throughout the country in the mid-1960s and in the vast majority of cases the objections counted for nothing. So it proved with the Cannock line and its neighbours at Walsall.

The Walsall - Dudley service was withdrawn in July 1964; the Dudley Dasher had ceased running the previous month. The last day for Burton-Lichfield-Walsall-Wolverhampton and Sutton Park line trains was Saturday 16th January. The Rugeley line had a two-hourly Sunday service, which ceased the following day, so on January 18th - Black Monday - only the Birmingham service remained. Even this had been reduced from half-hourly to hourly in 1963.

The Wolverhampton "Express & Star" reported the closures faithfully. The last train from Burton carried only a handful of passengers and was provided with a wreath by members of the Walsall Locomotive Society. On the Rugeley line the paper asked:- *"Will the passenger service ever re-open? If the answer depends on economics, No. Receipts, as Dr.Beeching would say,*

A Wolverhampton to Walsall push-pull train passes Walsall Gas Works, around 1955. The loco is an Ivatt 2-6-2 tank, possibly 41224.
(Roger Carpenter)

Ivatt 2-6-2T No.41279, shedded at Ryecroft, approaches Hednesford with a stopping train from Rugeley Trent Valley to Birmingham New Street, late 1950s. The Derby lightweight dmu is a sign that the old order was changing. The LNWR signal box dated from 1877. It had a 38-lever tumbler locking frame.
(Jack Haddock)

A member of British Railways' finest class of heavy freight locomotives, 9F No.92063, is seen between the LNWR Pleck Junction box and the new Walsall power box, summer 1965. The loco is sauntering tender-first towards Bescot, the right hand pair of tracks lead directly to the South Staffs line, the pair branching off them continue through Pleck to Willenhall and Wolverhampton. *(Jack Haddock)*

were nowhere meeting the 'true costs'. The last train down took 31 minutes without being pressed. It is scarcely a tribute to transport progress that the alternative express road buses will take 52 minutes."

With no previous experience of butchery on such a scale, opposition to rail closures all over the country was unco-ordinated, feeble and too late. After the South Staffs line closed the "Express & Star" noted:-

"Brownhills Urban Council is not letting the Beeching axe fall without a fight and is appealing to anyone suffering hardship by the closure, to keep a record over a few weeks, then send the details to the council." Beeching must have trembled at the thought.

It was not all bad news. A new freight depot had opened at Walsall in 1962. Bescot Yard was modernised and a new power box at Pleck Junction, Walsall was brought into use in March 1966. Together with the Down Tower box at Bescot, it covered an area of 21 route miles formerly needing 22 mechanical signalboxes. Most of the 72 running signals operated from Walsall Power Box were four aspect colour lights, 20 of which worked automatically ("Railway Magazine", February 1966). The line from New Street to Walsall was electrified, although it grudgingly petered out into just one platform at the station, like a trolley wire at the end of a rural tram terminus. A full electric time-table began in March 1967. The service became half-hourly again, with each fast train going via the Soho Loop and calling only at Bescot, which was even marketed as a park and ride station. The lone early morning train to Coventry via the Aston-Stechford line was also an emu, often a new Class 310 unit.

(This service was withdrawn in May 1990.) The only regular passenger train to use Walsall's non-electrified platform was a summer Saturdays working to Yarmouth. Dudley Freightliner Terminal opened on 16th July 1967.

Some of these improvements were short lived. Walsall's freight depot and the Freightliner Terminal are no more; Walsall-Birmingham trains were reduced to hourly again in May 1977 (restored to half-hourly in 1984) and the station buildings were demolished the following year. Well before then, efforts to re-open the Cannock line had begun.

A Long Campaign
In September 1970 Cannock Urban District Council initiated talks with British Rail and Staffordshire County Council to secure the restoration of passenger services. This was finally accomplished almost twenty years later, on Monday 10th April 1989. Those two dates were separated by years of wrangling, arguing, haggling and sheer frustration. Many communities throughout the country wanted their rail passenger service restored, but it actually happened so rarely that ground rules were almost non-existent.

The biggest question, which nobody wanted to answer was, "Who pays for it?" Sometimes, as with the Cannock line, one of the interested parties would finance a feasibility study and, depending on the outcome, events would proceed from there. I have had access to fifteen bulging files containing correspondence about the Cannock line campaign. Just one item summarises the situation admirably. Dated 31st October 1984, it is an appeal from the Railway Development Society asking

Park Royal dmus for Rugeley (left) and Birmingham New Street cross at Hednesford on 13th March 1963.   *(Peter Shoesmith)*

people to urge their county councillor to support re-opening:-

"Recently a 5,000 name petition was sent to Staffordshire County Council supporting the reopening of the line as a viable proposition which would bring new heart and life into the Cannock area. We are now on the verge of gaining this much needed rail service. A £20,000 study by British Rail has confirmed that the scheme is practicable and the West Midlands County Council have agreed to fund their share of the route. Estimates of usage indicate that the trains could well cover their costs and even make a profit! The three stations at Landywood, Cannock and Hednesford would cost £197,000 and Staffs C.C. have budgeted to spend this sum in 1985/6. The £197,000 for rail is a mere 1.3% of the £14,352,000 budget Staffordshire is to otherwise spend on new roads and vehicles in 1985/6. However, Staffordshire may yet have to trim its budgets and may therefore chop the rail scheme! If they do we may never again have the chance to open the Cannock train service. You must write now ...."

Further time was to elapse before the final piece of the jig-saw fell into place. Staffordshire County Council had to be persuaded that a decent rail service was an asset to the community, money they spent in support of it should be seen as an investment rather than a subsidy and - most important - those who needed the trains had the power to remind councillors that every so often they had to seek re-election. This they did on several occasions, notably at a well attended and lively meeting held in Hednesford on 16th November 1987. Discussions continued during 1988 until finally, in October, a financial package was agreed. The initial cost of re-opening was £500,000 - which would buy several yards of high quality motorway - of which £230,000 was contributed by the West Midlands Passenger Transport Executive (Centro) and £200,000 by Staffordshire County Council. The West Midlands County Council and, from 1986, its successor the West

Midlands Passenger Transport Authority, of which Centro is the administrative arm, has consistently and enthusiastically supported improvements to public transport infrastructure since the early 1970s. Throughout that decade there was an investment in greater integration between rail, bus and car, with a programme of improved rail services (eg; inauguration of the CrossCity service in 1978) better rail/bus links (eg; Shirley) and new or enlarged station car parks (eg; King's Norton, Stourbridge Junction). In more recent times, central government policy towards the rail network has been at best neutral and at worst openly hostile. It has lead to the lowest level of railway investment for any country in the European Union, perhaps best symbolised by the rundown in the rail construction industry - by mid-1996 not a single order for locomotives or other rolling stock had been placed with a British manufacturer by a British railway for three years! The policy of privatisation is being carried through despite overwhelming evidence that it is becoming increasingly unworkable and despite earlier spirited opposition from the few government supporters - most notably the late Robert Adley MP - who bothered to inform themselves of its long-term effects. Against this depressing national background WMPTA/Centro has invested in such significant rail developments as the electrification of the CrossCity Line (1993), and the opening of the Jewellery Line (1995), providing three new stations and a link through Snow Hill for the Stourbridge and Leamington/Stratford lines. In contrast, Staffordshire County Council had been less enthusiastic about rail improvements. Its £200,000 share of the Hednesford re-opening cost was not agreed without last ditch opposition by a small group of Conservative councillors. Once the service was running, many county councillors imagined that their task was complete. They thought that it could be forgotten, that it required no nurturing or support. This was not the case because, in the early days, the only unit

Despite other drawbacks, all the stations north of Walsall are fitted with ramps, intended to give disabled people easy access to rail travel. They are also ideal for mums with pushchairs, as proved by this happy picture taken at 'Babywood', which amply demonstrates one of the advantages the train has over the bus. A Tyseley based 'heritage' unit is arriving with the 10.41 to Walsall .
(courtesy of Mrs.Linda Bibb, from a photograph published in the "Evening Mail" on July 31st 1989)

available to work the Hednesford train was 30 years old unit and prone to failure. The central government policy of bus deregulation also meant that there were plenty of bus operators all over the country willing to offer artificially low fares in direct competition to local rail services. Within months of re-opening, a private operator was running buses every 15 minutes between Hednesford and Birmingham, without the burden of having to meet the 'track costs' of the roads they ran along. The days of integrating the different modes of transport for the benefit of all had gone. It was left to Centro to provide financial support of £100,000 per annum for the new service on the northern part of the line within Staffordshire (all transport authorities in metropolitan areas are allowed to support lines to a 'natural terminus' up to 25 miles outside their area if necessary). This support continues.

The Walsall-Hednesford line was opened in April 1989, with an hourly train service, plus a morning through train to New Street with an evening return working. The driver of the last train in 1965 had been Sid Hadley, by now in his eighties. By special invitation he enjoyed some cab rides over the route before the start of the new service. VIP and gala specials ran on Friday and Saturday 7th and 8th April, with a full public time-table commencing the following Monday. New stations were provided at Bloxwich (north of the original station), Bloxwich North (opened 2nd October 1990 after problems with land acquisition

were solved), Landywood and Cannock. The original up platform was refurbished at Hednesford (the down platform had been removed after closure) and a new crossover provided by Centro south of the station. The trains were to run on an experimental basis under the terms of the Speller Amendment legislation, a useful device introduced by Tony Speller, Conservative MP for North Devon, whereby a rail service can be re-opened to passengers (and closed again if unsuccessful) more easily than formerly.

The train service has been a success from the beginning. Within weeks of opening it was a common sight to see trains from Hednesford disgorging up to 200 passengers at Walsall. Landywood in particular was within walking distance for many young families; mothers with baby buggies could now easily travel to Walsall and rail staff dubbed the station 'Babywood'. Pressure of numbers meant that in October 1989 the frequency of Saturday trains became half-hourly in the run up to Christmas that year. An hourly through service between Hednesford and Birmingham began with the summer 1991 time-table. These trains were also able to call at Tame Bridge, which opened on 4th June 1990, alongside the busy Walsall Road, south of Bescot Yard. A large 233 space car park had been planned from the beginning, but prolonged difficulties with land aquisition meant that it was only constructed during 1996, after which the station was renamed 'Tame Bridge Parkway'. From the start of the 1996 summer time-table there was a fast train every hour linking all stations north of Walsall with New Street, calling only at Tame Bridge south of Walsall. In common with all other local services out of New Street, passenger numbers showed an increase in 1995 over the previous year. This was the only line which was busier on Saturdays than on weekdays, reflecting its use for shopping and leisure. All this success has been achieved with what is, in reality, a basic railway. This is in no way meant as a criticism of those who fought long and hard to see it re-opened or those who run it on a daily basis.

In the early days, when the 30-year-old Hednesford dmu failed, there was frequently no spare unit available, so the service was suspended. This happened so often that public confidence was dented and passenger numbers declined for a while. A low point was reached on Friday 5th October 1990, when most morning trains were provided by a new two-car Class 150 Sprinter, one car locked out of use because of a fault and the other grossly overcrowded on all journeys. It tottered into Walsall from Hednesford, just in time to find that the 11.05 connection to New Street had been cancelled. The ailing Sprinter failed in the station, as did its replacement 'heritage' dmu. A service of sorts was provided during the afternoon, but further failure caused it to be replaced by buses for the evening rush hour. All the stations are basic halts, never staffed and prone to vandalism. The life expectancy of replacement polycarbonate panels in the waiting shelters, at a cost of over £200 each, is short. At busy times it is difficult for the guard to move along the train to collect fares and revenue is lost. There is no full evening service and no trains at all on Sundays. Despite all these problems, the service has at last settled down, with a high proportion of trains running to time, due in no small measure to Centro's 'rewards and penalties' scheme negotiated with the train operator, which is now Central Trains Ltd. The line is now a successful and permanent feature of the railway passenger network.

The 1989 re-opening was always seen as a first stage; the real target was an extension to Rugeley and along the Trent Valley line to Stafford. At present the trains operate on a busy little branch line but this extension would plug Walsall into the wider passenger network. A simple journey to Stafford, for onward Inter City connections to North West England, North Wales and Scotland, would remove the need for Walsall passengers to travel in the wrong direction via Birmingham New Street first.

Services are set to return to Rugeley in 1997, eight years after they reached Hednesford and two years after Rugeley Town first appeared as a ghost station with no services in the all-line time-table. A financial package was finally agreed in August 1996 which would satisfy Railtrack, which is nationally responsible for charging rail companies and others for the use of the rail network. Railtrack is the infrastructure company created by the privatisation process and there has been much criticism of the high level of its charges. For example, they have caused - it is claimed - the cost of delivering rolling stock (eg; the final Class 323 electric multiple units, completed 1996) to be so great that it proved considerably cheaper to deliver them by road. Although such high charges had been levied for some years before Railtrack was formed, there is no sign as yet that the company wishes to ease the financial burden on potential users of its tracks - quite the reverse. The fact that the Hednesford service looks certain to be extended to Rugeley is a cause for both hope and despair, along with several other aspects of the current situation.

Some Ways Forward
The extended service, which will run hourly, will use a new down

Transrail liveried Class 56 No. 56 070, with a northbound mgr train, coughs extravagantly as the signal clears on the approach to Pleck Junction. The photograph was taken from the Wallows Lane bridge, with the disused South Staffordshire line to the right, 7th May 1996.
(Author)

Onwards to Stafford. A logical extension of the passenger service from Walsall, Hednesford and Rugeley, will be to Stafford, once more giving Walsall direct rail access to the northern half of Britain. The new service will reach Stafford via the Trent Valley line, seen here. The line from Hednesford and Rugeley Town comes in from the left. It is scarcely visible but no matter - any excuse to print this splendid shot! The up "Welshman" hurries on its way to Euston with "Royal Scot" 4-6-0 No.46142 "The York and Lancaster Regiment" in charge, 13th August 1949. The scene is framed by Rugeley Trent Valley's outer home LNWR 'skyscraper' signal gantry. A further gantry can just be seen to the left of the train, nearer the station, which lost its buildings and became an unstaffed halt in October 1972.
(E.S.Russell; Don Powell collection)

platform at Hednesford and a station at Rugeley Town, where it will terminate. It will *not* serve Rugeley Trent Valley just over a mile away, so there will still be no northern outlet for the whole Walsall and Hednesford line, even though the trains will run empty to Trent Valley in order to use the crossover there! Trent Valley station is a barren windswept halt, served only by Trent Valley line local trains, a virtually useless daily total of four trains in each direction (summer 1996 time-table). Yet the lighting and footbridge timbers have recently been renewed and there is a reasonable car park, sufficient to attract passengers from the cluster of prosperous villages north of Rugeley, such as Abbots Bromley, once there is an hourly service to Walsall, Birmingham and Stafford.

One of the unsung success stories of British railways in recent years has been the creation of new long distance secondary services. These include East Anglia - Nottingham - Liverpool and new flows on Trans-Pennine routes to Preston, Scarborough and Middlesbrough. Since at least 1990 the Hednesford line has been seen by Regional Railways (now Central Trains Ltd.) and Centro as part of a possible longer distance route linking Stafford, Walsall, Dudley, Stourbridge and Worcester. A glance at a map will confirm how useful this link would be, opening up a host of journey opportunities. Dudley in particular would benefit, as the town station would be near the Zoo and the Black

Country Museum, each of which has a marketing target of half a million visitors a year for 1997 and beyond. The line is now disused north of Brierley Hill Steel Terminal and the viaduct at Parkhead, over which the track has been lifted, requires attention before it can become a through route again. The viaduct is not irreparable and there is no serious opposition to the re-introduction of a train service.

In 1996 the agreed policy between the WMPTA and the metropolitan district councils local to the line - Dudley, Sandwell, Walsall - is for eventual restoration of a rail service. Part of the route, between Wednesbury and Dudley, would also be used by Line 2 of the Midland Metro, involving shared use of the tracks. A feasibility study will determine whether this can be achieved. Although radical-sounding, such a scheme is not without successful precedent, in Karlsruhe, Germany. Construction of Line 2 of the Metro is unlikely to begin for several years. If it is found that the two systems can operate together the rail route can bring benefits to medium and longer distance travellers in the area, while the more flexible Metro could better serve local needs. When leaving the rail formation at Dudley, for example, it would utilise street running to serve the town centre, which the train has never been able to do effectively. However, it would be tragic if the opportunity to improve public transport in Walsall - Dudley - Stourbridge corridor were not taken up. The unusual concept (for this country) of shared rail/Metro running, the fact that restoration of rail services is seen as a long term objective and the continuing shortage of capital to invest in such projects, are all factors which could inhibit progress. In my view, the best outcome would safeguard the route so that it could be used once more by passenger and freight trains, whether or not they share it with the Metro.

The Birmingham-Walsall-Hednesford service is now more frequent than ever before, with four trains every hour to Walsall, two of them fast via the Soho Loop and calling only at Tame Bridge Parkway. One of the fast trains provides the through service to Hednesford. Not surprisingly passenger figures, although too commercially sensitive for publication, are encouraging, although the service still needs financial support from Centro. The likely extension to Stafford could provide a stimulus which would increase the frequency of trains north of Walsall. In the longer term, the fourteen mile gap between Walsall and Rugeley would be electrified (highly unlikely in present circumstances) and there could be semi-fast trains linking Birmingham and (say) Manchester running via Walsall.

The diesel service between Burton, Lichfield, Walsall and Wolverhampton, introduced in 1958, was an idea ahead of its time. That time has now come. The road journey between Walsall and Wolverhampton, whether by car or bus, is slow and increasingly congested through much of the day. There is a seven-mile-long electrified railway linking the two, but no passenger trains have run on it since 1965. There can be no other pair of towns of comparable size and proximity in the whole of Western Europe which do not have some form of rail passenger connection with each other. As long ago as 1989, British Rail costed the relaying of a single track on the missing five mile section north of Walsall, between Ryecroft and Anglesey Sidings, at £4 million, less than a third of Staffordshire's road budget for a single financial year, 1985/6. Brownhills and Pelsall are similar in character to the Cannock area, with many young families and a lower than average level of car ownership. Both stations, if restored on their original sites, would be well placed to improve

the quality of public transport, saving 60% of the journey time between Brownhills and Walsall. An additional station has been proposed for the growing community of Clayhanger. Re-opening would also benefit freight traffic, as for many journeys it would once again provide a more direct route than the Sutton Park line. Each freight journey would represent a saving of 30 minutes in time and 15 miles in fuel consumption, which is a round average of one mile per gallon for freight locomotives. It would also relieve the Sutton Park line of some traffic, making it easier to integrate that line's restored passenger trains with its remaining legitimate freight trains. The trackbed between Ryecroft and Anglesey is safeguarded by Centro. There have been meetings since 1990 between various transport and local government bodies, such as Centro, Walsall MBC, Staffordshire County Council, Cannock Chase District Council. A feasibility study has been initiated by Centro in partnership with Walsall MBC.

Some developments in recent years, especially the steady increase in passengers and gradual improvements to the Birmingham-Walsall-Hednesford service, are causes for hope. The gathering momentum of the privatisation process, whilst unlooked for by local authorities throughout the country, can sometimes be turned to the potential advantage of the travelling public. For example, during 1997 WMPTA/Centro need to approve the Public Service Requirement and the franchisee wishing to operate train services in its area. I am given to understand that potential operators will be required by WMPTA not just to consider services within the West Midlands County, but to their terminal points, such as Rugeley, Lichfield, Redditch, Bromsgrove, Worcester, Shrewsbury. The authority will also ask potential operators to consider what can loosely be described as its "wish list", likely to include such items as the restoration of Sunday services, the provision of a Walsall - Wolverhampton service and extension of the Walsall-Rugeley service to Stafford.

These are interesting times for the lines which have been the subject of this book; it will take time to see whether or not they are allowed to develop in a way that will serve the area to the greater benefit of its people.

Taken from the photographer's back garden, summer 1962. The unidentified Stanier Black 5, with a rake of non-corridor stock, is approaching Willenhall with the last passenger train of the day, around 7pm, between Walsall and Wolverhampton. There is no hint of litter or debris in the cutting. This part of the original Grand Junction line has seen no regular passenger services since 1965, although it is now an electrified freight route.

(Bob Lane)